CW01023283

'It's very rare in a subject as cr⌐
to find a book that feels imm
Elizabeth Harrin's book is that ⌐
understand not only how to run
way that ensures your project w
and the people within it.

It's a wonderfully crafted little book...Elizabeth Harrin has articulated the role, responsibilities, tasks, challenge and excitement of working in project management in a way that made me want to be able to restart my career all over again.'
Jonathan Norman, *Manager, Major Projects Knowledge Hub*

'Elizabeth Harrin is superbly up to the task of introducing the field of project management to both newcomers and project veterans alike. As a former PMO lead and PM instructor, I found Elizabeth's work highly engaging. Not only does she present the foundational aspects of project organization in an accessible way, but she also offers a human angle that other texts sorely lack...Buy *Project Manager* today!'
A. Geoffrey Crane, *Trent University*

'Elizabeth has another winner on her hands with her latest IT focused project management book *Project Manager*. This is a must have for any new project managers wanting to learn about the role, understand best practices and get brought up to speed on all the latest tools, methodologies and industry terms...Great book, and a must buy for every project manager!'
Bill Dow, *PMP, ITIL author of The PMO Lifecycle: Building, Running, and Shutting Down*

'This is a wonderful book. I wish I'd read this 25 years ago when I started managing software projects. Seriously. So much of this I learned the hard way by doing, and this book is straight forward, easy to read and covers all the bases. Nice job Elizabeth!'
Monica Borrell, *Founder and CEO, Cardsmith*

'A clear, comprehensive introduction to IT project management that will suit anyone starting out as an IT project manager, whilst being broad enough to have plenty of interest for the more experienced.'

Richard Newton, *award winning author of* The Management Book *and* The Management Consultant

'*Project Manager* is the perfect tasting menu for any would-be project manager in the IT sector. It'll give you a flavour of the whole discipline, familiarising you with all the jargon, the principle methods, and the kind of career you can expect. Like any tasting menu, it leaves you wanting more of the best bits, and wondering 'just how do they do that'. If you're about to start a career in IT project management and don't have someone to answer all your questions, here's what you need. Ask Elizabeth and she'll tell you the answers.'

Dr Mike Clayton, *CEO & Founder, OnlinePMCourses.com*

'This is a great guide for anyone beginning their career in IT project management or wanting to move into the industry. Guidance on when to use agile methodologies and the importance of aligning IT projects to business strategy sit alongside a comprehensive overview of the role, responsibilities and tools of the IT project manager.'

Caroline Harper, *Corporate Lead ICT and Digital, South Tyneside Council*

'This is great book for anyone who is interested in becoming an IT project manager...As an accidental PM who knows that you can have a really good, rewarding career in project management, I found this book ideal for anyone who has thought that project management may be the right path for them and would highly recommend it.'

Donna Unitt, *Head of Delivery, Rocket Consulting Ltd.*

'Elizabeth Harrin's new book *Project Manager* is a valuable resource not only for anyone who wants to start a career as an IT project manager but also for established project managers wanting to refresh the role...Elizabeth's' natural and genuine writing feels more like peer advice received over a cup of coffee than a technical reference manual, and makes for an interesting read with plenty of good advice to consider.'

Rebecca Gordon, *Director, Programme and Project Capability Building, Australian Federal Public Service*

'A must-have for every project manager... The book works for those who are looking to embark on the exciting journey of becoming a project manager as well as seasoned project managers and everyone else in between. It also serves as a great reference guide, giving you those essential tips and pointers to ensure that your projects have the best chance of success.'

Raj Sharma, *Consultant Senior Project Manager*

'A go-to source for those interested in what being an IT project manager is like. It particularly addresses the key concern of today's project manager with ensuring that projects – especially those delivering tech solutions – actually deliver real business benefits, and also the challenges of aligning the proven advantages of agile approaches with the fulfillment of over-arching strategic objectives. A 'day in a life of an IT project manager' chapter helps to bring it all to life.'

Bob Hughes, editor and co-author of *Project Management for IT-Related Projects*

''Elizabeth's latest book is as practical and applicable as we've come to expect from this experienced author.'

Penny Pullan, *Director, Making Projects Work Ltd*

'Another pragmatic publication from Elizabeth to help those starting out in their careers in project management.'

Peter Parkes, *Programme Director, Peak Performance Consulting and author*

PROJECT
MANAGER

BCS, THE CHARTERED INSTITUTE FOR IT

BCS, The Chartered Institute for IT, champions the global IT profession and the interests of individuals engaged in that profession for the benefit of all. We promote wider social and economic progress through the advancement of information technology science and practice. We bring together industry, academics, practitioners and government to share knowledge, promote new thinking, inform the design of new curricula, shape public policy and inform the public.

Our vision is to be a world-class organisation for IT. Our 70,000 strong membership includes practitioners, businesses, academics and students in the UK and internationally. We deliver a range of professional development tools for practitioners and employees. A leading IT qualification body, we offer a range of widely recognised qualifications.

Further Information
BCS, The Chartered Institute for IT,
First Floor, Block D,
North Star House, North Star Avenue,
Swindon, SN2 1FA, United Kingdom.
T +44 (0) 1793 417 417
www.bcs.org/contact

http://shop.bcs.org/

PROJECT MANAGER
Careers in IT project management

Elizabeth Harrin, MA, FAPM, MBCS

Published by BCS Learning & Development Ltd, a wholly owned subsidary of BCS, The Chartered Institute for IT, First Floor, Block D, North Star House, North Star Avenue, Swindon, SN2 1FA, UK.
www.bcs.org

Paperback ISBN: 978-1-78017-4167
PDF ISBN: 978-1-78017-4174
ePUB ISBN: 978-1-78017-4181
Kindle ISBN: 978-1-78017-4198

Ebook available

British Cataloguing in Publication Data.
A CIP catalogue record for this book is available at the British Library.

BCS books are available at special quantity discounts to use as premiums and sale promotions, or for use in corporate training programmes. Please visit our Contact Us page at www.bcs.org/contact

Publisher's acknowledgements
Reviewers: Peter Parkes and Raj Sharma
Publisher: Ian Borthwick
Commissioning Editor: Rebecca Youé
Production Manager: Florence Leroy
Project Manager: Sunrise Setting Ltd
Cover work: Alex Wright
Picture credits: Image from Shutterstock by Jules_Kitano
Typeset by Lapiz Digital Services, Chennai, India.

CONTENTS

LIST OF FIGURES AND TABLES

FIGURES

TABLES

ABOUT THE AUTHOR

Elizabeth Harrin, MA, FAPM, MBCS is an author, copywriter and content marketing strategist for project management firms. Elizabeth also works as a practising project and programme manager. She spent eight years working in IT for financial services (including two based in Paris, France) before moving into healthcare. Elizabeth has over 10 years' experience in healthcare technology, and she has worked on large-scale IT implementations including introducing new radiology systems to over 30 hospitals and leading the implementation of a new enterprise resource planning (ERP) system across the business. She currently leads compliance and business change projects.

Elizabeth is a PRINCE2®, MSP® and P3O® Practitioner, and holds the ITIL® Foundation certificate. She is a Fellow of the Association for Project Management and a member of the Project Management Institute (PMI). She holds degrees from the University of York and Roehampton University.

She is the author of five books about project management: *Communicating Change, Shortcuts to Success: Project Management in the Real World* (which was a finalist in the Management Book of the Year Awards 2014 and is now in its second edition), *Collaboration Tools for Project Managers, Customer-Centric Project Management* and now this one. Elizabeth has also written several ebooks.

She's particularly interested in stakeholder engagement and team communications and how these affect project outcomes.

Elizabeth is the award-winning blogger behind A Girl's Guide to Project Management (www.girlsguidetopm.com), a specialist project management blog aimed at helping people manage their projects with more confidence and less stress. She is widely published on project management topics and has contributed to numerous websites and magazines. She speaks at conferences internationally.

You can find Elizabeth online at www.girlsguidetopm.com or:

- Twitter: @girlsguidetopm
- Facebook: facebook.com/girlsguidetopm or in the Project Management Café group: facebook.com/groups/projectmanagementcafe (come and join us!)
- Pinterest: pinterest.com/girlsguidetopm

ACKNOWLEDGEMENTS

I'd like to thank Frances Place, Emma Seaton-Smith, Donna Unitt, Glen Alleman, Deepesh Rammorthy, Mayte Mata-Sivera, Sarah Johnson, Aaron Porter and Elise Stevens for allowing me to share their stories.

Thanks also to Dovilė Misevičiūtė at Eylean for the screenshots of Agile tools, Monica Borrell at Cardsmith for the screenshot of a Kanban board, Steve McConnell and Construx Software Builders, Inc. for permission to reproduce the cone of uncertainty, Lindsay Scott and Nadine Rochester at TwentyEighty Strategy Execution for allowing me to adapt and reuse some blog articles for this book, and to Rebecca Youé and the BCS team for asking me in the first place.

I'm also appreciative of the thoughtful comments provided by the two reviewers, who took their own time to provide helpful feedback about how to make this book better. Any oversights and omissions are most definitely my own.

Finally, thanks as always to the team at PACE Computer Training for their ongoing support in so many ways. Love you!

ABBREVIATIONS

API	application program interface
APM	Association for Project Management
BA	business analyst
BCS	BCS, The Chartered Institute for IT
CAB	Change Advisory Board
CAPM®	Certified Associate in Project Management
ChPP	Chartered Project Professional
CMDB	configuration management database
CPD	continuous professional development
DSDM®	Dynamic Systems Development Method
ERP	enterprise resource planning
IPMA®	International Project Management Association
ITIL®	Information Technology Infrastructure Library
M_o_R®	Management of Risk
MoP®	Management of Portfolios
MoV®	Management of Value
MSP®	Managing Successful Programmes
P3O®	Portfolio, Programme and Project Offices
PgMP®	Program Management Professional
PID	project initiation document

PMI	Project Management Institute
PMO	Project/Programme/Portfolio Management Office
PMP®	Project Management Professional
PRINCE2®	Projects in a Controlled Environment
RACI	responsible, accountable, consulted, informed
RASCI	responsible, accountable, supportive, consulted, informed
RPP	APM Registered Project Professional
SFIA®	Skills Framework for the Information Age

GLOSSARY

Agile   A way of delivering projects that encompasses various approaches and methods that are incremental, iterative and with a strong focus on delivering prioritised user requirements.

Burn-down chart   A way of displaying progress and value delivered in Scrum and agile project management.

Change management   The way we facilitate the shift from current practice to new practice in order to achieve a benefit.

Configuration management   The discipline of having control over who is doing what to what, and which version is the most current. Involves creating, maintaining and managing changes to the products you are delivering.

Dependencies   The way tasks link to each other on a project schedule – for example, tasks needing to be completed in sequence or in parallel.

Development team   Self-organising, cross-functional team responsible for delivering the work at the end of an agile iteration.

Gantt chart   Horizontal bar graph showing project tasks and their duration.

Handover   The process of passing what the project has delivered to the operational teams who will be responsible for managing and supporting it once the project is closed.

Kanban   An Agile approach using visual planning to manage project tasks.

Portfolio The sum of all projects and programmes being carried out in an organisation department, or division, often including business-as-usual activity too.

Product Owner Key member of the Agile project team; the main project stakeholder. The person responsible for the requirements and priorities for the project.

Programme A group of related projects that often use a similar group of resources and will together achieve an overall common objective or set of related objectives.

Project A unique series of activities that together have a common goal and that must be completed within a defined timescale, a specific budget and to a defined specification.

Project board A group of people who form the decision-making body on the project, including the project manager, project sponsor, key supplier and other senior managers who hold particular influence over the resources, budget or success of the project. Also known as a 'steering group'.

Project management The management framework and activity required to get a project going and to keep it going until it achieves its agreed objectives.

Project sponsor The person accountable for the successful delivery and benefits of the project through the realisation of the business case.

Release The distribution of a version of a software product. Normally refers to making the new version 'live' in the production environment.

Retrospective A meeting held at the end of an iteration on an Agile project, to reflect on what worked and consider lessons to apply to future iterations to improve the way the team is working and the outputs.

Scrum An Agile framework for getting work done using sprints.

Scrum Master A servant leadership role that supports, coaches and mentors the Scrum team.

Stakeholder   Someone who is affected by, or has an interest in, or believes they have an interest in, the delivery and outcomes of a project.

Standard   A document produced by the consensus of a group of experts and approved by a recognised body. It includes the rules and guidelines aimed at helping individuals and teams deliver consistently and in a structured way – for example, *A Guide to the Project Management Body of Knowledge (PMBOK® Guide)* – sixth edition (a standard from PMI).

Waterfall   A non-Agile way of managing project work where the requirements and scope are defined as fully as possible at the outset.

PREFACE

You're interested in becoming an IT project manager? You're in the right place. IT project management is a fascinating and highly rewarding career choice.

This book is especially for you. We lift the lid on the role of the project manager and tell you what it's really like. You'll discover the background and context that will help you decide if the role of an IT project manager at any organisational level is a good fit for your career aspirations. And this book will tell you what it takes to be successful in these roles.

Project management can be the beginning of your career journey if you decide that this is the job for you. Later on in the book we look at the different options open to you for growing a successful (and well-paid) career, through the different certifications you can study for and how you can move on from project management if you decide to take your career even further.

HOW THIS BOOK IS ORGANISED

Each chapter includes information about a different aspect of IT project management as it relates to the role.

Chapter 1 covers the basics of project management and IT project management in particular.

Chapter 2 looks at the role itself, covering the competencies, skills and behaviours of successful project managers, the responsibilities of the job, and the context of the environment IT project managers work in.

In **Chapter 3** you'll learn about the different team structures and interfaces to key people and teams within the project.

Chapter 4 talks about how work gets done. You'll find out about the tools, methods and techniques that project managers use every day.

Chapter 5 covers career progression – everything from finding your first job to leaving project management after (hopefully) many successful years and moving on to bigger challenges.

Chapter 6 is a day in the life story from a real IT project manager so you can see what a typical 12 hours on the job is like.

Throughout the book you'll see real-life stories from people who are in the role of an IT project manager. From the radiographer and electrical engineer who found career paths into IT, to experienced technical experts, you'll read case studies about how other people secured jobs, chose their qualifications and developed outstanding careers in this exciting discipline. You will see this anecdote icon in the margin to focus your attention on these real-life stories:

 ANECDOTE

An anecdote or case study; real-life experience from leaders who have faced these situations and taken purposeful action

Each section ends with a summary of the key points, further resources and an invitation to share the subject with your social network. Use the hashtag #itpm and be sure to tag @girlsguidetopm so my team and I can share too.

1 INTRODUCTION TO PROJECT MANAGEMENT

This chapter defines what a project is and looks at what project management delivers. You'll learn the differences between project work and business-as-usual work, and see why an understanding of your company's strategy in the widest sense is going to help you be a success as a project manager.

By the time you've finished reading through this chapter, you'll know all about why project management is a highly valued skill within IT and you'll be in a good place to decide if it's a career that sounds interesting for you.

WHAT IS PROJECT MANAGEMENT?

Businesses never stand still. If you want your company to move forward, you've always got to be tweaking a product line or introducing something new. These changes help keep your business competitive and ensure that you can deliver your company's strategy.

Strategy is what drives businesses to change. Whatever your strategic themes and objectives – to be the market leader for something, or to be your customer's first choice or to be incredibly profitable – you aren't going to get there by doing the same things you are doing today. Strategy underpins the changes that your business makes in order to get to where you want to be.

The changes that a business needs to make in order to deliver strategy are called projects. Projects can deliver small changes or contribute to major business transformation.

To be sure we're all talking about the same thing, this is a good place to define a project.

A project is a unique series of activities that together have a common goal and that must be completed within a defined timescale, a specific budget and to a defined specification.

Projects are different from the day-to-day activity of the organisation because they have a defined start, a middle and an end. They are pieces of work with parameters fixed by their very nature, and while they might deliver an ongoing service, such as a new product line, the project itself will close down once this is complete.

This makes projects distinct from business-as-usual tasks as you can see from Table 1.1.

Table 1.1 The differences between project work and business-as-usual work

Project work	Operations
Changes the business	Identifies the need for change
Defined start and end date	Ongoing
Often involves mainly capital expenditure; can be difficult to budget due to unknowns	Costs are normally taken in the profit and loss accounts; budget fixed for the period
Often involve cross-functional, multi-disciplinary teams brought together on a temporary basis	Mainly delivered by line or functional teams who work together permanently

(Continued)

2

Table 1.1 (Continued)

Project work	Operations
Manages risk to deal with uncertainty and to take calculated decisions	Mitigates risk to remove uncertainty from business operations where possible
Does something new	Does repeatable work
Planned around business need with time, cost and scope constraints	Operational, often annual, planning cycle

HOW IS PROJECT MANAGEMENT DIFFERENT FROM PRODUCT MANAGEMENT?

Great question. And there is often a degree of confusion between the two terms. As we've seen, project managers are responsible for the successful delivery of a project, as a one-off piece of work. Product managers are responsible for the life of a product.

A project might produce a product, and the product manager will be on the project team. But then the project manager walks away ... and the product manager stays. The product manager ensures the product is successful. They may initiate other projects to improve the product in the future. They work with customers to define how the product should evolve, and they develop any strategies around the product. Eventually, they decommission the product when its useful life ends (and that might be another project).

The easy way to distinguish between the two roles is that the product manager provides continuity for the product. The project manager is involved for the duration of the project.

Businesses can have any number of projects on the go at the same time, depending on their size and the resources they have available.

A **programme** is a group of related projects that use a similar group of resources and have a similar overall objective (to become a paperless business, for example).

A **portfolio** is the sum of all projects and programmes in the business, department or division, and often includes elements of business-as-usual operations too.

Programme and portfolio management give you the tools to scale what you do on projects and gain efficiencies in how work is managed. These are looked at briefly in Chapter 5 in relation to how your project management career might develop, but they are really outside of the scope of this book – we're focusing here on managing projects.

Projects don't just happen by themselves. **Project management** is the activity required to get a project going and to keep it going until it achieves its objectives or is closed. Project management involves:

- removing roadblocks so other people can do what they need to do to hit the project's goals;
- planning, monitoring and controlling projects;
- getting work done through and with other people to deliver a goal;
- making sure projects deliver the objectives on time, on budget and to the required quality.

In other words, project management is getting things done in a sensible, structured way.

Project management is not:

- purely an admin role;
- telling people what to do all the time;
- ticking off tasks on a list;
- following processes and expecting everything to work out for the best.

What is a project manager?

Project managers use project management to make things happen.

As we go through this book you'll understand more and more about how project managers contribute to the business overall by shaping and delivering the work with the project team.

WHAT HAPPENS IF A PROJECT CAN'T ACHIEVE ITS OBJECTIVES?

It would be great to think every project delivered exactly what was expected, but that doesn't happen in real life. Objectives can change, especially if the organisation's strategy takes a different direction. For example, you might need to scale back a project or extend the scope. It's highly likely that what you deliver at the end of the project is different to what was set out in the original business case, but as long as all the project stakeholders agree to the changes, that's OK.

The other thing that might happen is that the project is closed before it reaches the planned end point. It's more common than you might believe for a project to stop prematurely. This can happen for lots of reasons. For example:

- The senior manager who started the project leaves the organisation and no one else thinks the project is worth continuing.

- The business strategy changes and the project no longer fits with the new strategy.

- The project takes too long or costs too much and management decides to stop the project as there is no longer an adequate return on investment.

- It becomes clear that the project will never achieve what was hoped for and the decision is taken to stop throwing money and resources at something that won't deliver anything of value.

If this happens on your project, your role becomes to close down the project, move the project team on to other projects and salvage anything that can be used from what work has been completed so far. It's also important to learn and record what happened so that future projects don't end up in similar situations.

WHAT IS IT PROJECT MANAGEMENT?

IT project management involves taking the principles of project management and applying them in an IT context.

This normally means delivering IT solutions and working in an IT environment, either in a permanent, agency or contract role. Projects could involve infrastructure, platforms, security, software or anything in the IT estate. Even changing a switch could be managed as a small project.

However, the vast majority of 'IT projects' have a business element as well. We rarely implement technology for technology's sake and projects should be initiated to support a strategic business objective. You might be rolling out a software update, but that ensures the organisation has a safe and stable infrastructure from which to serve customers. Customer service and business continuity are the larger goals; the technology helps ensure that they can be achieved.

Here are some projects that might look like IT initiatives but that have an impact outside of the IT department:

- PC refresh: Staff need training on new interfaces, hardware and applications. The switch over should be planned with operational requirements in mind so there is minimum disruption to working patterns.

- Change to information security policies: Implications for staff need to be investigated as there might be the requirement to get users to sign to say they have read and understood the new policy, or handbooks in other divisions need to be updated, or existing contracts may need to be refreshed. Users need to receive some level of communication about what it means for them and when they will see new pop-ups amongst other changes.

- Telephony upgrade: Staff training might be required to deal with the change to a new telephone system, especially around accessing previous call recordings or reports. Downtime needs to be managed carefully to avoid operational impact.

For that reason, it's wrong to think of IT project management as a stand-alone discipline. At worst, doing IT projects in a way that is considered disconnected from the rest of the organisation leads to a 'them and us' mentality where IT is somehow separate from the rest of the business. This attitude breaks down relationships and results in decisions being taken that are not always in the best interests of the organisation as a whole.

What is an IT project manager?

An IT project manager is someone who works within the IT division of a company, leading and managing projects that have a large IT or technical element, or those being led (or sponsored) by the IT department. The role can involve different things in different organisations. Here are some examples of the kinds of projects IT project managers would be responsible for:

- An IT-led initiative for a purely technical project, such as looking at upgrading network switches across the global estate.

- The IT workstream or sub-projects within a larger business transformation project or programme. In this case, they would work as one of many project managers or workstream leads on the project, but would be responsible for the IT elements of the project.

- A project being sponsored by IT with a large business change element, such as a PC refresh or software development. As much of the work is technical, the IT project manager may lead the project but work with colleagues from across the business to ensure the project is managed with a 'whole business' approach and that change management is carried out effectively.

IT project managers look at their IT projects in the context of the wider business decisions. It's also essential to look at those projects in the context of the business strategy. Let's look more at that now.

Why project managers should care about business strategy

IT projects should underpin the company's strategic direction and support the business objectives – this is a fundamental part of a project's business case, which is how projects get started.

No matter how small or informal, every project should have a business case that sets out why the project is important for the organisation, and that's where you should see the link to the strategic objectives.

It's important that IT project managers understand the corporate strategy and work in a way that is aligned to that as much as any other division of the business would be. There are hardly any projects in the IT arena where business acumen and an awareness of your business context, operating environment and priorities will not help you do your work more effectively.

There has been a major shift in project management over the last couple of years towards an increased focus on strategic alignment and delivery. It isn't just a discussion for the senior leaders in your organisation. Project managers should be aware of and care about their company's corporate strategy. Today, project management isn't simply about delivering what you've been told to deliver and letting everyone else deal with the rest of it. Being able to connect your project to the company's goals is important, and here's why.

Reason #1: because outcomes matter

For too long project management has been focused purely on outputs.

> Outputs are what we call the products or deliverables created by a project – for example, a new smartphone app for car sharing. Outcomes are the difference made by the deliverable: the change we get as a result of the output. In this example, the outcomes would be fewer cars on the road, easier commutes to work, lower pollution and new friendships made on the drive.

It's old-style thinking to believe that projects deliver outputs and that it's someone else's job to think about how to use those to get any benefits out of the work and into the organisation. Project managers who want to actually contribute to the business need to do more than simply deliver what they have been asked to. They need to make the connection between their deliverables and the outcomes they facilitate.

Business savvy project managers – the ones who are winning awards and doing great things with their careers – are the ones who are doing this.

As a project manager, you aren't in the position to be able to deliver, track, manage and integrate benefits your project delivered, say, over the next five years. And it isn't your job to do this over the long term. You'll be whisked off to a new project before the (virtual) ink on the project closure document has dried. That's the pace of business; there's always a new project to do.

But that doesn't preclude you from being business-aware during the project. You can ask the right questions. You can make sure that the business case that initiated your project is watertight and that you keep going back to it. You can ensure that there is a benefits plan that sets out what the project's outcomes and benefits will be. You can check that the right people know how and when those benefits will be realised, how they are going to track them over time and what to do if it looks like they aren't getting the benefits they expected. You don't need to know all the answers; you simply need to ask the right questions.

Additionally, you can recommend solutions, and if they change, you can propose how your project changes to keep pace with new technology. You can add tasks into the project schedule so that business owners find it easy to measure their outcomes. You can check that your project is still worthwhile at every key decision point. You can guard the project's money like it's your own and invest it wisely. You can challenge. You can even propose that your project is closed down or paused if something else comes along that has a more positive business benefit. You have a lot of power to make sure that your project does everything it can to get those outcomes.

And you should, because it's part of your role to help the business be successful.

Reason #2: because it helps secure support for your project

Being business savvy helps you secure support. It's an easy sell when you can tell a senior stakeholder that their involvement in your project will help deliver some portion of business strategy or it underpins a strategic pillar of the organisation. If you're trying to convince them to turn up to a meeting because your sponsor has told you to invite them, that's far harder. We'll look more at the interfaces between the project manager and others in the organisation in Chapter 3.

Knowing the strategy helps you frame your requests in ways that are more likely to build support for your project and get the right decision for the business overall.

Reason #3: because it builds morale

People like to know that they are contributing to something worthwhile. Linking your project to organisational strategy in a way that your team members can understand helps them see the part they play in the bigger picture.

You may have come across Maslow's Hierarchy of Needs,[1] which is a motivational theory. Maslow identified five levels of 'needs' that humans are motivated to achieve. Social needs relate to the sense of belonging: playing a part in a project team can fulfil this, but it helps even more if you can meet Esteem needs. These relate to achievement and recognition. People often feel like their achievements will gain more recognition if they are working on a strategic initiative or one that can be linked to the organisational direction, because it's perceived to have more management oversight and exec support (which is probably the case).

Linking what your team members do to the context of organisational strategy is an easy way to build morale and show your team that they are contributing to the bigger picture in a worthwhile way.

It's also easier to convince people to make a pivot if it's in the interest of organisational strategy. Teams tend to understand why something has to pause or resources have to be reassigned if they can see the big picture influence. 'Because my boss asked for it' isn't a helpful answer when you are trying to keep the morale of the team high during difficult times.

Reason #4: because it's good for your career

Finally, we shouldn't overlook that being aware of business strategy is good for your career.

Being able to talk about your project in terms that relate to strategy and organisational context will set you apart from the next project manager. In the main, executives don't care much about dependencies on a Gantt chart or your beautiful resource tracking spreadsheets. They care about the bottom line, hitting shareholder targets, what the markets think and how they are going to get the next massive project done while still keeping the profit and loss accounts balanced. They care about sticking to the strategy.

Someone who can communicate in ways that speak to those drivers will stand out – and this goes for anyone in any role, not just a project role. The fact is, though, that project managers often have more knowledge of strategic initiatives and more influence over senior execs than other team leaders in the business simply because of the work they do and the company they keep. In a project management role you have plenty of opportunities to impress; don't waste them.

Underpinning all of this is the fact that you have to know what the business strategy is. You can't support or deliver to something if you don't know what it is. If you aren't sure, find out how your project fits into your programme or the longer term plan. Spend a little time understanding what your business is going through and where it wants to be. It will be a lot easier to see where your project fits into the big picture and how your IT project management role is helping to get there.

Emma Seaton-Smith moved into IT project management from a clinical background working as a radiographer. Below she explains how she made the transition.

After my first degree in jewellery design, I researched the possibility of doing Graduate Entry Medicine, but I was excited by radiography and the visual element of beautiful images really attracted me. I wanted to combine these interests and apply them in a very practical profession.

I was a radiographer for nearly a decade. I wouldn't use the cliché of 'I fell into IT project management', but there was a gap in the needs of a changing business where I picked up the slack. The medical imaging company I worked for was bought and as a radiography manager there, I took on a key role in integrating our radiology imaging IT systems into the parent company. I also worked through each of the hospitals in the parent company to get them live with our imaging service.

When my role was made redundant, the parent company took me on in a project manager's role. It was a job role I'd seen others doing and aspired to. I hadn't realised how much my skills were valued, so I was thrilled when it was offered.

I completed the PRINCE2® qualification soon after I started my IT role. As a new project manager it helped me to become familiar with the elements of a project and formalise my processes and documentation. I learned the language of the profession, which is a fundamental tool in any career.

Project management is transferable across so many different industries, so even if you move on, the skills you learn will be invaluable to any job role you do in the future.

Emma Seaton-Smith, UK, healthcare technology

SUMMARY

Project management is the activity required to get a project going and to keep it going until it achieves the agreed objectives or is closed. It's what a project manager uses to ensure a project has the best possible chance of being successful. IT project managers take the principles of project management and apply them in an IT context, although understanding the business strategy for any project will make you more successful at delivering it.

Do this

Find a project manager within the IT division of your company and invite them for coffee or a chat to find out more about IT project management in your business. If you aren't working at the moment, try to find a local networking group near you (there's more on professional bodies in Chapter 5 and many of them run events) so you can chat to some people who currently do the job.

Watch this

The history of project management in under 3.5 minutes. This short video from the Association for Project Management shows how far project management has come: https://youtu.be/5nrlwYRs5Ko

Share this

IT projects underpin the company's strategic direction #itpm

Project, programme, portfolio: do you know the difference? #itpm

2 THE ROLE OF THE IT PROJECT MANAGER

This chapter looks at the role of the project manager in an IT organisation. It's a big chapter and it covers:

- why the role exists;
- what makes a top performing project manager;
- the competencies and soft skills required to succeed in the role (technical skills, processes, tools and methods are covered in Chapter 3).

The term 'IT project manager' and 'project manager' are used interchangeably.

By the end of this chapter you will have a good idea of the behaviours, interpersonal skills and personality traits that will help you do well as an IT project manager. But first, let's start with an awkward truth.

THE TROUBLE WITH BEING A PROJECT MANAGER

There's one small problem with being a project manager.

If the work goes well, the team says: 'Why did we need you? We did a great job.'

If the work goes badly, the team says: 'You weren't a very good project manager.'

The skill in project management (aside from not taking things personally) is making the work look and feel effortless even when a lot of planning has gone into it to get to that point. Good project managers unblock tricky situations for their teams, smooth over the office politics and give people the tools and environment they need to do their best work.

Project managers are the planners, the organisers, the communicators behind the scenes, but they don't get involved in doing the tasks. You can schedule the unit testing, but you won't be unit testing yourself. You'll record, monitor and track project risks but you won't take steps to mitigate the risks yourself – that's the responsibility of someone in the team.

However, another common challenge for people in a project management role is that they are expected to do the tasks in the project as well as manage the project. They often have the skills to do so, having moved into project management from a development or team leader role in another IT function. Project management is sometimes part of a role rather than your whole role and in that case you'll have to switch between your 'doing' hat and your 'project management' hat. Even if project management is supposed to be your whole role, you'll find yourself helping out with the tasks from time to time because it's sometimes unavoidable – for example, if someone is sick or on leave. Look out for when these activities are taking so much effort that you don't have time to do the project management aspects of your role.

You will find the role of a project manager hard to explain to others at parties. You will find that your family don't really know what you do all day (but you could give them this book as a starting point). But project management is the most rewarding and fantastic career, even when you're knee deep in a project crisis that no one saw coming.

THE OBJECTIVES OF THE PROJECT MANAGER'S ROLE (OR, WHY THE ROLE EXISTS)

The role of project manager exists because time after time studies show that a structured approach to getting work done is a better way to get successful outcomes than rushing around not knowing what you are supposed to be doing. A methodical approach to identifying what needs to be done, planning the work and carrying it out is far more likely to give you good results than a slapdash approach.

It's not rocket science but it's also not simply common sense, or the amount wasted due to poor project performance wouldn't be as high as 9.9 per cent of every dollar. That equates to $99 million for every $1 billion invested in project work.[2]

Executives have for some time seen the value in employing people to manage temporary endeavours (projects) just like they employ people to manage permanent parts of their businesses (functional teams).

The objectives of a project manager's role are straightforward.

A project manager balances time, cost and quality to deliver something of value to the organisation.

If you can do that, then you will be more likely to succeed in the role and have a positive impact on your organisation.

Figure 2.1 Balancing project constraints to deliver value

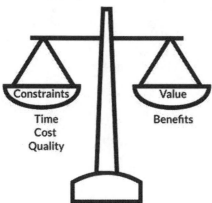

WHAT IS PROGRAMME MANAGEMENT?

Project management and programme management are often confused.

A programme is a collection of related projects, all with similar aims, objectives and resources that together deliver a common outcome or a significant change; for example, moving the company to being a paperless office would be a programme with a number of projects such as:

- choosing and implementing an electronic document management system for head office;

- designing a paperless sales process for use in the company's shops and implementing it to all branches;

- launching an employee portal for electronic payslips and HR information;

- launching an electronic expense management system with approval workflow.

And so on.

Each of these is a project with a project manager, but together they deliver a transformative change for the business. The overall change is managed as a programme, under a programme manager who will consolidate programme-level risks, manage resource conflicts across all projects, control the budget and work with business owners to realise the benefits across all the initiatives.

Programme management requires a different skill set from that of project management, but it's often considered as a future career move for experienced project managers. This book doesn't comprehensively deal with programme management skills, although they are discussed briefly in Chapter 4. You'll find some skills do overlap with project management skills.

WHAT MAKES A TOP PERFORMING PROJECT MANAGER?

In this section we'll look at the skills you need to be a top performing project manager. It's a long list. You'll find that thought leaders, recruiters and professional bodies all have their own opinions of what 'good' looks like for the skills of a project manager. There is no single definitive list of all the competencies you need for success. This is a good thing, because it gives you the flexibility to develop all-round skills for business success, and to use the approaches and skills that work best for you in your environment.

The professional body view

There are a number of professional bodies that accredit and certify project managers. These organisations have defined what competencies are required to successfully carry out the project management role. However, having a certificate doesn't automatically make you a top performing project manager. Certifications give you the foundation of skills and knowledge, and a platform from which to develop further.

Table 2.1 looks at the main professional bodies active in the UK and the main competencies they assess for project managers, based on my interpretation of the syllabuses and exam content outlines provided for their major relevant certifications. There is further information on professional bodies and the standards, methods and tools they support in Chapter 5, and contact details for each in Appendix 1 so you can dive deeply into their frameworks.

The depth of assessment of soft skills in different exams varies, and that's not surprising. It's hard to assess soft skills in an exam environment, and project management courses traditionally have focused on the technical and method-driven skills such as planning, scheduling and estimating, which are critical for successful projects. These best practices are discussed in Chapter 4.

19

Table 2.1 Main professional bodies and competencies they assess

Qualification or competencies	Professional body		
	BCS, The Chartered Institute for IT	APM, Association for Project Management	PMI, Project Management Institute
Qualification	IS Project Management Higher Certificate (v. 6.4 syllabus)	PMQ (Sixth Edition syllabus)	PMP (Exam Content outline, June 2015 edition)
Communication	Y	Y	Y
Leadership	Y	Y	Y
Teamwork	Y	Y	Y
Stakeholder management	Y	Y	Y
Supplier relations	Y	Y	Y
Conflict resolution	Y	Y	Y
Negotiating	Y	Y	Y
Coaching, mentoring, training			Y

PRINCE2® is excluded from Table 2.1. Neither PRINCE2® nor AXELOS (the company responsible for developing, enhancing and promoting it) are professional bodies. PRINCE2® is a method and, as such, leadership and interpersonal skills are specifically excluded from the guidance.

Whether you join and abide by the framework of a professional project management association or not, there are some skills and behaviours that all successful project managers have in common. Let's look at these now.

Seven essential competencies for project managers

Project managers are good all-round players, often with domain knowledge in the area where they are working (such as infrastructure, platform or digital). The job requires a degree of structure and organisation plus great people management and the ability to engage others in the work. Consequently, the list of skills, behaviours and competencies you need to succeed in the job is incredibly long. As you surf the internet and read into the role of the project manager you'll see different skills make it to the top of each researcher's list.

Drawing on my years of research, experience and interviews with project managers, here's my take on the seven essential competencies for those who want to succeed in the role.

1. People-orientated

Great project managers are people-orientated. That doesn't mean you have to be an extrovert. It does mean that emotional intelligence, being able to 'read' people, being good at building relationships, listening and showing empathy are important skills to develop. A natural interest in connecting with people helps too.

These characteristics are top of the list because your project is changing how other people do their jobs. Big projects such as IT outsourcing may even be putting them out of work. You need to be aware of the consequences of your actions and how this can affect other people.

Project management firm Systemation profiled hundreds of project managers over a decade and their study shows that people-orientation is the top aptitude required for project managers.[3] Fewer than 14 per cent of the project managers chosen to go through the Systemation assessment

21

programme scored low on people-orientation. Those that didn't show aptitude in this area struggled to build successful working relationships and had difficulty getting the most out of their teams. In many cases these project managers were reassigned to other positions where they could contribute to the business in ways that more accurately played to their strengths.

2. Teamwork

Along with being alert to the challenges of working with others and aware of how people are acting around you, project managers are most successful when they enjoy working as a team. Your project team are the people you will spend most of your time with – not other people in project management jobs. This can sometimes feel isolating as you don't have anyone around you day to day working in the same role as you – projects only need one project manager – but if you can draw energy and enthusiasm from your team then that's going to help you succeed together.

Being a team leader can be a challenge, as projects don't always go smoothly (more on that later). You'll need to be able to work with the team even when it's tough, which means taking the lead in dealing with conflicts, navigating office politics and handling the personal situations of your team members with discretion and grace.

3. Communication

Being able to communicate goes hand in hand with being a team leader. Your team will be more successful if you can create an environment whereby information is freely shared and communication channels are open both among themselves and with others.

Great project managers are aware that communication is about more than just pushing out your messages. You have to make sure that they are received, understood and acted upon. Plus it helps to have a feedback loop in place so that you are listening to what your team and project stakeholders are telling you as a result of your communication.

Project managers need to be able to effectively communicate:

- in person, on a one-to-one basis, in a small group such as a team meeting and to a larger audience such as giving a presentation to the department;

- in writing, such as in emails, project newsletters or other project documents;

- at a level that your audience can understand – for example, presenting technical detail to the IT security team but providing a higher level overview for departmental managers.

This is something you can practice. The more you build communication into your project plans, the easier you will find it. Encourage your team to communicate too, and lead by example by sharing all the information you have from your senior project stakeholders or project sponsor that is not confidential.

4. Self-confidence

Often in projects you are treading paths that no one has gone down before. It helps to have a degree of self-confidence in your abilities when doing something new.

However, no one wants to work with someone who is arrogant. Self-awareness will keep your confidence in check and ensure you don't tip off the end of the assertiveness scale and fall into the mistake of being arrogant.

Having confidence in your abilities doesn't mean you'll never have to ask for help. Recognising your own strengths and weaknesses is definitely part of being self-aware. Be prepared to ask for help if you need it and surround yourself with people who are strong in areas where you are not so strong. Overall, this will help you balance the team and ensure that together you are able to deliver what's needed for the business.

5. Strong desire to achieve

Project managers have a strong desire to achieve and are motivated by completing work. You may feel that this is a natural fit for your personality and that in your life in general you are goal-orientated and highly motivated by achievement.

You don't have to be naturally this way inclined to succeed as a project manager, although it helps.

This competency is all about staying focused on the goal. As a leader, and as a team, you cannot waver from that. Losing focus can result in many problems including:

- missing deadlines;
- overspending;
- bloating the project scope through uncontrolled changes;
- failing to deliver any benefit.

And, ultimately, losing focus could result in the project being closed down and considered a failure.

Staying focused on the big picture and always linking current activities back to the big picture is something that successful project managers do regularly.

6. Ability to remain calm

Projects don't always go to plan. In fact, it's highly likely that you'll hit problems on your project. Customers change their minds, someone goes off sick, the technology doesn't perform as you expect or a supplier lets you down. There are loads of reasons why the path of your project is going to be challenged and it's your job as the project manager to deal with these situations.

Being able to stay calm in a crisis is a great skill to have because your attitude and behaviour rubs off on your colleagues. If they see you dealing with a crisis in a calm way, they'll act accordingly. If you are rushing around in a panic because a vendor has just made a multi-million-dollar mistake in the code, they'll panic too.

You are, of course, entitled to panic in a crisis, just don't let anyone on the project see you do it. Talk to a trusted colleague, your Project Management Office (PMO) or mentor if you need support in the first instance. The team look to you to guide them through difficult times.

7. Flexibility

When things don't go to plan on your project you need to be able to pivot and flex as required, *and* bring your team along with you.

You may need to flex your approach because your project sponsor changes their mind about what they want to do or because some external constraint means you have no choice but to take a different direction.

Whatever the cause, when you've spent a long time working on a project schedule, and your team have prepared estimates that feel realistic and relate to the work at hand, having to change direction can feel uncomfortable. In a traditional project environment, changes can mean a lot of rework and building new relationships. They can mean going over your schedule line by line and working out what needs to be changed and how that is going to affect your ability to deliver the project's objectives.

Changes are always welcome in Agile ways of working, even late in the process, but you'll still need to be flexible in order to incorporate them.

Changes happen for lots of reasons and being able to roll with the punches will make the experience of managing a project far more pleasant for everyone. The project manager who sticks to the schedule despite knowing it will no longer deliver what is required will quickly find herself out of a job.

MANAGING MEETINGS

There are a lot of meetings on projects. One of the key skills for a project manager is being able to chair a meeting *and* get the results required after the meeting.

As a project manager you need to be able to:

- Organise and set up the meeting for success: ensure there is an agenda and that everyone has a copy; book a room or meeting space and tell people when they should be there, including dial-in details for virtual meetings.

- Manage introductions, and open the meeting, setting the scene by explaining why you are all there and what you hope to get out of the meeting.

- Move the attendees through the agenda on time and purposefully, covering all topics in the appropriate level of detail – especially important in virtual meetings.

- Deal with any other business raised during the meeting, either in the meeting or by recording it to discuss another time.

- Record minutes and actions (or work with a colleague who is doing this on your behalf) and distribute those.

- Follow up on the actions, ensure everyone completes the tasks they were assigned.

If you have access to a project support officer, project coordinator or a member of the PMO team, you may be able to use their support to do some of these tasks. Use them if you can.

Agile teams meet daily in 'stand up' meetings, run by the team. These are often constrained to 15 minutes and focus on individuals reporting:

- what they accomplished since the last meeting;
- what they'll be working on between now and the next meeting;
- what's blocking them from moving forward.

The project manager can attend these meetings but wouldn't be asked to set them up or chair them. The meetings are a fast way to ensure the team is making progress. And yes, attendees at stand up meetings do stand up – removing chairs from the setting is a good way of keeping people focused and meetings short. If you need deeper discussions, these can be had outside of the daily stand up.

While meetings on an Agile team might look different some of the time, there will always be occasions when your job requires you to work with others who have a more traditional outlook on meetings and want chairs!

Project managers need a wide variety of skills to succeed in their roles. Experienced project manager Donna Unitt explains what she thinks is important below.

We've moved away from the project manager as the person sitting in the corner updating Gantt charts. Today it's all about engaging people: building rapport, understanding their issues, the politics and the challenges and getting a feel for what they want to get out of the project. Spending time with stakeholders helps you build trust.

In IT project management it's not the technical side that's most important. It might have been like that once, when people came into the role from a pure IT background, but it's not the case any longer. Now it's about being organised, driving the work forward, communication and engagement. You don't need to be in the weeds: we need to look at projects holistically and don't need to understand every nuance of the technology. I'm interested, for example, in when a deliverable is going to be ready and how long it's going to take to get there. Couple that with thinking about how people are going to adapt and use the new system when they get it: I'm interested in how it's going to get used and the benefits as well.

Be clear in your role, what you need and why it is important for the team to work efficiently. One colleague wanted to know why I was chasing him all the time. When I explained it was because I wasn't getting the information I needed, and why I needed the information, something clicked and he understood. I don't want to micromanage my team, but I do need to be able to track and report the project.

Part of my role is educating others about why we need to follow a methodology, how our processes set us apart from our competitors and how much customers value the repeatable and proven approaches we take to deliver consistently and minimise risk.

Donna Unitt, UK, supply chain consultancy

Additional desirable skills

On top of those critical skills, project managers need a rounded approach to managing the work and a wide variety of interpersonal skills. Here are some additional skills that good project managers demonstrate. They are secondary in that you can manage a project without them, but they certainly make life easier and are worth cultivating over time if you do not feel you are particularly strong in these areas.

Creativity

Project management might not look like the most creative of jobs on the surface. You're often given the project on a plate and told to deliver 'that' using tried-and-tested processes and methodologies.

However, creativity is a fantastic skill to have for problem-solving and dealing with issues. Getting your team together and helping them to think outside the box is the fastest way out of difficult situations. When the team hits an issue, the project manager's role isn't to solve the issue alone, but to gather some potential courses of action, review the options and help the team come to a conclusion about what would be the best route forward.

Using your problem-solving skills and thinking creatively about issues can help you and the team come up with better solutions.

Organisation

A good project management methodology can offset some of your own natural disorganisation but you will perform better as a project manager if you are naturally organised (or if you can be organised if you try hard enough).

Being systematic in your approach to work will really help you stay on top of things.

Delegation

One of the unique things about the project management role is that you're not responsible for the doing of the tasks. You might read that part of a project manager's job is to allocate or assign tasks to others.

In reality, that's done based on discussion and taking into account team members' skills, experience and interest. In Agile methodologies, teams are self-organising and members get to choose the things they would like to work on from the backlog of tasks.

Scrum teams choose upfront so they each know what their responsibilities are during the sprint (the defined period of work, called a timebox, like a project phase – there's more on Agile methods in Chapter 4). Kanban and Scrumban teams choose as they go.

Project managers do, however, have to be able to work with the team to make sure that the right work is done by people with the right skills, and to get people to take responsibility for the ownership of that task. While it's great to give your team as much autonomy as possible, you can't fail to deliver on your project goals simply because no one much fancies working on that task this month. Your skills at delegating morph more into making sure all the tasks are being picked up and that nothing is slipping through the cracks.

In some cases, your team will need you to specify exactly what it is that is expected from the task for the project. Being able to give clear instructions about a task, provide full information and give others what they need to be able to complete the work is an important skill.

Influencing and negotiating

Project teams come together for a defined period of time and it is most likely that the project team members will not work for you directly. They will have line managers back in their functional teams, and their project work will either be on a full-time secondment or part-time basis but they won't officially leave their 'home' team. There's more on the different structure of teams in the next chapter.

Managing people who don't work directly for you is a challenge. They will have split priorities and split loyalties. They've effectively got two bosses – more if they are working on several projects. It can be hard for them to prioritise and to balance the competing needs of the different endeavours that they are involved with.

Being able to influence others and negotiate for the resources you need on your project are key skills for a project manager. You'll use these both with your team members and also with their managers.

If you don't feel particularly confident in your ability to influence and negotiate with others then don't worry: these are definitely skills that you can develop and improve with practice and training.

Administration

You can't escape the fact that when you start out in a project management role (and even when you get to be quite senior) you'll be doing a lot of updating logs and project documents and other project admin yourself. If your company has a PMO or project coordinators, you may be able to use them to help with project admin, although you'll still remain accountable for it.

There is a lot of paperwork in project management, and while you'll use your professional judgement to tailor your methods and approaches to fit your project, you still need to be aware that there's a big chunk of admin to do.

Good computer skills will definitely help, and you should be able to use word processing packages and be comfortable with spreadsheets for managing project budgets.

It's also important to be able to find the files you have created. So much time is wasted looking for documentation, so being able to store your documentation in a way that suits the IT systems you are using will save you many headaches later on.

Finding ways to highlight decisions made (a simple log of decisions, who took them and why, will do) and important artefacts so that you can quickly get back to them will also be very useful.

Attention to detail

This might seem contrary to the points earlier in this section that project managers have to be focused on the big picture to get the team across the line and deliver what's expected. While that's certainly true, there is a big part of the project manager's role that involves paying close attention to the details. Often when a detail is overlooked, something breaks along the chain which puts the bigger picture in jeopardy.

For this reason, you'll often see project managers with detailed project schedules and 'To Do' lists, covering tasks that other people are responsible for doing. By tracking details, they can make sure that everything is covered and that things are moving in the right direction.

Leadership

Finally, being able to lead your team is important for project managers.

Note that leadership is different and distinct from management. Management is being able to organise work, plan, structure activities and follow through. It involves executing tasks, following processes and controlling the work. Leadership has more to do with getting others to understand the vision, sharing the goals and getting people to follow you there, motivating them to do their best work to help you achieve those objectives.

We've already seen that teamwork and being people-orientated are key skills. It's also important to be able to act in a leadership capacity, guiding the team to the goal, even if you aren't in a traditional leadership position.

Experienced project manager and coach Elise Stevens believes leadership is a key skill for IT project managers. Below she explains why.

The one skill you really need to have is to be a good leader. You have to demonstrate positive leadership. Instead of trying to jam people into roles that don't fit them, use the people you have to do what they are good at. This comes from understanding your team and working as a team.

Being a leader means leading across vendors and cross-functionally as well to get the best results. Stakeholders might have responsibility for driving outcomes but you need a good rapport and relationship with them – which extends to telling them when they need to do something (and giving them enough notice to do it).

> IT complains that there is a big divide between 'the business' and IT. Being a good leader is about working together. Think about how you can lead this project so that everyone involved is travelling in the same direction and engaged along the way, so you are working as a team in the truest sense.
>
> *Elise Stevens, Australia, consultant in*
> *utilities and other industries*

WHERE DOES A PROJECT MANAGER'S AUTHORITY COME FROM?

So how does the project manager get the authority to do all of this? Authority refers to your ability to make decisions about project planning, task execution, resource allocation, spending the project's budget, approving work and similar activities.

In many jobs, your authority is linked to who you work for. If you work directly for the CEO, mentioning their name opens doors and confers a degree of authority on you. That's not how project management works.

Often, your line manager will be the functional manager in charge of all project resources, or perhaps a head of department. While they might be important in the organisation, your authority to run a project isn't linked to them.

Your authority to manage the project comes from the governance structures around the project. The initial project documentation – the project charter or project initiation document – will include a list of people who will work on the project and your name should be on there in the role of project manager. This document is approved by the relevant senior business leaders and your project sponsor. The fact that they have approved the work to be done and your role in the work as the project manager, gives you the authority to proceed.

If you are not sure how much authority you have, you can always check with your project sponsor. However, as the saying goes, it's easier to ask forgiveness than permission. You know your organisational culture, but in many cases, as long as you are acting with the project's best interests at heart, you can go ahead and take action.

ETHICS: AN UNDERPINNING SKILL

Being able to operate ethically is important for all roles, and project management is no exception. Given the amount of emphasis on leadership, stakeholder and relationship management and the impact that transparency, honesty and integrity can have on building a successful team, ethics is essential for today's business.

PMI has a Code of Ethics and Professional Conduct for project managers.[4] APM also has a Code of Professional Conduct[5] and whether you are a member of those bodies or not, it's worth familiarising yourself with the standards to which project managers should hold themselves accountable.

Codes of professional conduct set out the standards for how project managers should behave. They cover personal responsibilities and responsibilities to the profession. Dealing with grey areas in the ethics arena isn't a common problem for most project managers but certain cultures and industries will expose you to more dilemmas than others. Generally speaking, in an office-based, UK-based IT role, you are unlikely to be asked to take a bribe in exchange for awarding a contract or anything similar, for example.

However, it's important to be aware of what might be an ethical grey area so that you can take advice as appropriate and not put yourself or your business in a difficult position. Here are some pointers for ensuring you manage your project within the boundaries of professional ethics.

1. Disclose any interests you have

Conflict of interest is one of the more common ethical dilemmas, especially in smaller, well-connected industries, or where you have personal contacts in the same industry.

For example, if you have personal connections to the company putting forward a proposal during supplier selection you should definitely let your project sponsor know. It would be best for you to take a step back from the procurement work so that you can't be accused of making a decision that is in the best interests of a family member or friend.

2. Don't reuse assets from your last job

It's common practice to reuse templates and project documentation to make the most of what you have and avoid duplication of effort on every project. But if your old company had a fantastic set of design principles for websites, you can't get them out, rebrand them with your new company's logo and start putting them in front of clients.

Don't reuse assets from your last job. If nothing else, they are probably protected, with proprietary intellectual property (IP), and your old contract may have specifically outlined what you can and can't do with company property.

You can't unknow what you know, so you can use your interpretation and your knowledge to create a set of design principles allied to the values of your new organisation but informed through all of your professional expertise. It's quite likely you were hired because of the experience you gained elsewhere but you have to be careful about how you make use of this in any new role.

3. Don't leave information out deliberately

This is lying by omission. You can get round difficult questions by failing to include the one piece of information that wasn't technically asked for but that might change everything.

For example, if you are asked if your project is on schedule, you could reply: 'Right now we're sticking to the plan'. That gives the client the impression that all is well. However, if you know that there is a huge risk coming round the corner that's probably going to push you off course next month then you've deliberately left out information that would give them the complete picture.

This isn't honest or transparent. It's giving your clients a poor service and doing a disservice to your team as well.

4. Be brave

Stand up for what you believe in. Don't be afraid to call people out on their behaviour. If you hear someone making offensive remarks, say something. Don't be bullied and don't let other people be bullied either. This is where your leadership skills can make a real difference.

Whatever your values are, stand by them – and even if you can't quite articulate them you'll know when you see or are asked to do something that just doesn't feel right. Life is too short to compromise on what is important to you.

5. Challenge decisions

You should always feel that your sponsor is open to hearing your opinions about the project. You have been trusted with delivering this piece of work on their behalf and they owe you the time to listen to your opinion if you think something is going off track.

If you feel that a decision has been made that isn't the right thing for the project, challenge the decision. Talk to your sponsor about why you feel like that. They may well overrule you and go with what they want to do anyway, but you'll have had your chance to make your point and you may well be able to convince them that an alternative path is better.

Never let the fact that someone is in a more senior position than you stop you from speaking up when you have a legitimate dissenting view. However, you'll need to be aware of the political and strategic context of your project so that you can discuss it carefully, and in an articulate and professional way.

6. Don't ask your team to do unpaid work

Everyone on your team loves their job so much that they would come in and work on the weekends for free just because they hate being away from the office so much, right? Perhaps there are workplaces like that, but you'll find that there is a limit to your colleagues' generosity when it comes to putting in extra effort for your project.

Project work isn't a Monday-to-Friday, 9 a.m.-to-5 p.m. job, and most people will understand that if you take the time to explain to them what's required throughout the project life cycle. It's common for the workload on projects to be a bit 'up and down' – when there is a release or the project launches is always a busy time, for example.

However, there are limits. Requiring people to do unpaid overtime isn't acceptable.

If they volunteer for whatever reason, then that's different. But don't pressurise them or 'encourage' them to do more than they are prepared to do. They have responsibilities to their families and they have bills to pay. Be respectful of their time and their capacity to earn.

7. Don't play favourites

Humans are social creatures. While we are drawn to making friends, you'll find that not everyone falls into the 'potential friend' category. The good news is that you don't have to *like* everyone at work. You just have to be able to work with them. A professional, respectful relationship is all that's required.

The bad news is that if you do have close friends at work, your relationship with them could come across as favouritism, even if you are trying really hard to avoid that. Fairness is important in teams as it helps create trust and mutual respect. Don't take a junior colleague out to lunch once a week because you're turning into great friends and then ignore the others in the team. If you can't treat all your staff fairly, don't create situations where you are treating them differently. Perhaps do your lunches on rotation, so everyone gets time with you as their project manager and mentor.

Working within ethical boundaries is not difficult: it should be part of the fabric of who you are and how you work. Your professional values will be tested on complex projects. In summary, do all you can to make sure that you stay within professional boundaries and never put yourself in situations where you feel you could compromise the project, your reputation or your organisation.

A PROJECT MANAGER'S RESPONSIBILITIES

The sphere of control for a project manager is what you are responsible for. This might be clear from your job description, but it's more likely to be something you grow into, your responsibilities changing as your project sponsor gains confidence in your abilities to do the job.

You will be able to take on more and more responsibility as time goes on and you develop skills and experience.

Regardless of your past experience, when starting a new project it's always a good idea to confirm your sphere of control with your project sponsor or line manager. This ensures that you know your boundaries and the area in which you can operate.

Project managers are typically responsible for:

- initiating the project;
- planning the project;

- monitoring and controlling the project's performance and taking corrective action as necessary as the work progresses;

- achieving the goal while staying within pre-defined parameters for time, cost and quality;

- closing the project at the appropriate time.

The extent to which you'll be able to achieve all of these, and your freedom of operation within these areas, depends on what you have agreed as part of your role and your level in the organisation, which we will look at more below.

Setting your boundaries

Have a conversation with your sponsor about setting boundaries before you start a project. Make sure you know what environment you are operating in and how much influence you can have over this.

Set and understand your boundaries as early as you can in the project. There are two main elements to doing this.

Firstly, it's important to know how much latitude you have on your project to make decisions and to shape how the work is done. For example, you don't want to be in a position where you make a decision not to use a certain tool only to find that this has repercussions downstream for others in the business who rely on that tool for data. You may not have any ability to change the method used, or how you tailor it to suit your project. Conversely, there might be plenty of scope to adapt standard templates or make decisions about how to carry out the work. Discuss this with your project sponsor or line manager so you know what the constraints are in terms of project management approach.

Secondly, it's important to be clear on tolerances specifically for this project. Tolerances are how much you can flex within your project without having to go back for approval, specifically around budget and schedule but you can also set them for other areas. There are some examples in Table 2.2.

Table 2.2 Example project tolerances

Area	Tolerance level	Explanation
Budget	+/- 10%	As long as you are within 10% of your forecasted budget at completion you can carry on. As soon as you are forecasting to spend more than 10% you have to alert your project sponsor.
Schedule	+/- 10 days	As long as you are forecasting to complete the project within 10 days of the scheduled end date you can continue without seeking further input. If the forecasted project completion date stretches to more than 10 days after the current baselined schedule date, you need to seek approval from your project sponsor.
Risk	None requiring sponsor involvement and/or fewer than five risks with 'Major' status	As long as there are no risk management actions that need sponsor involvement, or fewer than five risks with the status of 'Major', then you have the freedom to continue to manage these within the project as long as they are reported in the monthly project reporting.

Tolerances are useful because they mean you don't have to continually go back to your project sponsor to ask for permission to complete the project a day late or a few pounds over budget. Defining your tolerances, and then managing to them, gives you and your sponsor the ability to set criteria around what you can and can't do on the project.

These tolerances are specifically about how you will do project management on the project – they relate to the boundaries you have around how you are managing the work. You can also set tolerances for the outputs of a project. For example, if you are launching a new web-based service, you may have tolerances for quality defined in your quality criteria such as:

- website loads within 0 to 0.7 seconds;
- website page size is between two and three megabytes;
- auto password recovery email is sent within one to two seconds.

It is important to manage your work so that you know when you are approaching your tolerance limits, and what you should do when that happens. As soon as you know you are going to breach a tolerance, you should escalate this to your project sponsor and let them know.

You may also find that from time to time an event occurs that would keep you within your approved tolerance but that you think your sponsor should know about. Professional judgement always trumps arbitrary rules, so if you think you should inform your sponsor of something, then go ahead and do so.

Understanding a project manager's responsibilities at different levels

What a project manager is responsible for differs between companies, industries and individuals as your experience and skills clearly influence what you can and can't do in a project environment.

Luckily there is a benchmark for what a project manager should be responsible for at different levels within an organisation.

The SFIA® (Skills Framework for the Information Age)[6] framework is the most comprehensive definition of IT skills in global business. It's regularly updated by the SFIA® Foundation so it stays relevant, which is particularly important given how fast-moving the IT industry is. At the time of writing, SFIA® version 7 has just been released.

How SFIA® works

The framework is made up of skills and tasks at different levels. It defines a common language about skills, abilities and expertise across technical roles. It's used by individuals and organisations across the IT industry and at varying points in their career development to plan development activities and inspire career progression.

There are seven levels of responsibility in the framework, from Level 1 (an entry level, working under direction role) to Level 7 (the most senior level in an organisation with responsibility for things like policy and formulating strategy).

Project management responsibilities kick in at Level 4, so you couldn't carry out the role of a project manager at a level below that.

SFIA® outlines six skills categories:

1. Strategy and architecture
2. Change and transformation
3. Development and implementation
4. Delivery and operation
5. Skills and quality
6. Relationships and engagement.

Project management is a skill in the change and transformation category, but there are many elements of a project manager's role that could fall into the other areas.

Below we'll look at some of the common responsibilities for people carrying out project management at different levels in an organisation, as set out in the SFIA® framework. The framework does not give job titles at each level, but I have provided them to give you a reference for the kind of job that you might be doing at each level.

Responsibilities for a project manager (SFIA® Level 4)

In this role you'll work under the general direction of someone else and within a clear framework of accountability. You'll know where your boundaries lie and what scope you have for taking decisions on the project and on behalf of the team.

You'll be able to work largely autonomously with a substantive degree of personal responsibility for the work, the team and the deliverables of the project. You are responsible for planning your own work, filling your day with the relevant tasks and using the right processes to get the job done in a way that meets the objectives for the project.

You'll be responsible for:

- Defining, documenting and carrying out small projects or sub-projects such as the IT workstream of a larger business project. This generally means working on initiatives that are up to a year long, with a limited budget that you may or may not be directly responsible for. Smaller projects have limited interdependencies with other projects, and often have a small or no significant strategic impact. You could be working on a project alone or with a small team and you'll be responsible for project work across all phases of the project from initiation to completion.

- Identifying, assessing and managing risk.

- Agreeing the project approach with stakeholders. In other words, how you will get the project done and what tools you'll use to do so.

- Preparing realistic plans for the work. Project plans cover more than just tasks and the dates when work will be done (we call this plan the project schedule). You'll also prepare plans to cover the activities required for managing risk, quality and stakeholder engagement and communication.

- Tracking activities against the project schedule.

- Managing stakeholder involvement in the project as appropriate, involving those who need to be involved at the right time and to the right level.

- Monitoring the project budget, timescale and resources and taking action where these deviate from the tolerances you have agreed with your project sponsor.

- Formally closing down the project when the work is delivered and reviewing, recording and sharing the lessons learned.

Responsibilities for a senior project manager or programme manager (SFIA® Level 5)

In this role you'll work under your own initiative most of the time. You'll receive broad direction from your leadership. You are responsible for planning and scheduling work and you'll also assign tasks to other people.

You'll be responsible for:

- Defining, facilitating and completing medium-scale projects, including setting the approach. These projects will have clear deadlines and direct business impact.

- Identifying, assessing and managing risks that might stop the project being successful.

- Ensuring that the project plans are realistic and up-to-date, and in line with the methods used. For example, if you are using Agile methods, that your planning reflects this and that the tools are being used to the best advantage. You'll also take action if the project's performance starts to depart from the path that you have agreed with your project sponsor and other key stakeholders.

- Ensuring that there is regular communication with the stakeholders, and that this accurately reflects what is going on.

- Ensuring that quality reviews take place effectively and at the right time.

- Managing the change control procedure for the project.[7]

- Ensuring that project deliverables are completed within the parameters agreed around budget, resource and schedule, and that deliverables are handed over to users and signed off.

Responsibilities for a portfolio manager or project office manager (SFIA® Level 6)

In this role you are most likely responsible for a team of project and programme managers, or you head up a division with a significant amount of project management work, or perhaps you are the PMO manager or a project sponsor. Depending on the organisation and project, you could also find project managers leading significant, strategic, critical and complex projects at this level.

Positions at this level carry a significant amount of influence over strategic direction and policy.

You'll be responsible for everything mentioned in the levels above, and more, including:

- Taking responsibility at the highest level for the successful completion of complex projects. These projects would have significant high-profile impact, political sensitivities or business criticality with high-risk dependencies.

- Choosing the methods and tools for projects or the division.

- Ensuring that all project management best practices are followed including effective change control and risk management.

- Monitoring and controlling all aspects of the project including operational and capital expenditure and any impact on revenue.

- Managing the expectations of everyone on the project from executive sponsors to end users, including suppliers and other relevant third parties.

Responsibilities for a projects director (SFIA® Level 7)

Someone in this kind of role, operating at this level, will be one of the executive team. This is probably the person who has ultimate accountability for projects within the business, such as the projects director, strategy director or similar. Job titles can vary between organisations and some businesses may not have someone responsible for projects operating at this level.

In these kinds of positions, the individuals involved will be setting strategy and policy related to project management, programme management and portfolio management across the organisation.

You'll be responsible for:

- Creating the organisational strategy relating to project management. This could include mandating appropriate tools, standards and methods.

- Authorising large projects and overseeing their management.

- Leading strategic projects that are considered high risk or have a significant impact. This could translate to operating in a project leadership or sponsorship role, and wouldn't necessarily mean that you were doing the hands-on scheduling, monitoring and controlling of the project.

- Ensuring compliance to processes like change control and making sure that issues are being addressed in line with standards and processes.

There's a lot to consider at every level. The role of the project manager has wide-ranging responsibilities but there are some threads around planning, monitoring and control that you'll see throughout the levels.

Regardless of your position in the organisation, the role of a project manager in the IT field can be incredibly varied. Deepesh Rammoorthy, a project manager in the healthcare industry, describes how a chance encounter can be an opportunity to demonstrate customer service whatever level you work at.

Yesterday I went to donate plasma and the nurse there found out that I was working for the Blood Service. As soon as I said I was from the IT department, she showed me her laser printer that was crinkling the pages and indicated that she had called up support but got no answer.

Being aware that after hours support is only provided to cover systems that have broken down and does not cover non-essential items like printers, I explained this to her. I confirmed that there was another working printer for them to use. When I got into work the next day I also advised the Support Desk to look out for the query.

It's very important to know not only your stakeholders but your organisation's customers and also to clarify what service your department can offer them and when. It is important for an IT Project Manager to develop business relationships. It helps to be able to explain the Service Catalogue – essentially the services that IT can provide to assist and enhance business processes. We need to be able to explain how IT can be a real partner with other business units, working hand-in-hand as a business enabler and not simply being the scary acronym that only tech savvy people can understand.

Deepesh Rammoorthy, Australia, healthcare

SUMMARY

Project managers make a contribution to the way change is delivered, because a structured approach helps to get work done effectively and efficiently. Project managers need a wide range of skills and competencies to be successful in the role. The responsibilities of a project manager differ from business to business, and depend on the level at which you operate. Professional certification schemes assess knowledge and behaviour, and provide a foundation for further development.

Read this

Overcoming Imposter Syndrome by Elizabeth Harrin: A short ebook about building self-confidence at work – helpful if you are feeling daunted about all the skills you're expected to have as a project manager (www.girlsguidetopm.com/overcoming-imposter-syndrome).

Project Management for Humans by Brett Harned: An easy-to-read and practical book that explores the relevant skills for project managers especially in a digital or Agile environment (but still a good read for everyone else too).

Do this

If you don't yet have a project management certificate, ask your employer what support they can offer you to get one. If you aren't currently working, look at what certification schemes are most appropriate for your level of experience and make a decision about which, if any, to go for.

Share this

This month I'm working on [insert skill]. What about you? #itpm

What project management certification do you have? Has it helped your career? #itpm

Take it further

Benefits management is an interesting, and advanced, topic. While it's not strictly the remit of a project manager, it can help to have some understanding of how benefits are created, realised and tracked. There are a lot of materials available on the discipline of benefits management, so dive into some of the many books available if this is an area that interests you.

3   PROJECT STRUCTURES

This chapter looks at the way IT project teams are structured within an organisation. We will cover the different team environments in which project managers work and the people with whom project managers work.

By the end of this chapter you will understand common team structures and the common roles that make up project teams.

COMMON TEAM STRUCTURES

The organisational structure of a company influences how you manage your project and the culture and environment you operate in. It also makes a difference to the amount of authority you have in your role.

There are three common organisational and team structures that you'll find in project environments: functional, project and matrix. As a project manager, you could work in any or all of these over your career.

Functional

A functional structure is one where the work is contained within a single department. In the IT arena, this could be a switch upgrade at the data centre which has no impact on other teams within the business. A project manager within a functional structure has the least authority over the resources involved in doing the work – they will report to their line managers as normal.

Functional structures have plenty of advantages: it's easy to get hold of the subject matter experts as they work in the same division as you, and conflicts can be resolved by going up the line as everyone reports into the same leadership team.

Projects run in a functional way within a department tend to have simple communication lines. If you hit a problem it's easy enough to resolve them with the skills you have in the group. This kind of project is a fantastic development opportunity for members of the department so you'll often have enthusiastic team members who want to learn. It's also a lot easier to hand over the deliverables at the end of the project, because the department is both the delivery team and the receiving team.

However, as with all team structures, there are disadvantages to working this way, not least in terms of keeping focus on the goals when there is strong loyalty to the department or functional team. When the department needs to focus on the next crisis or business-as-usual activity, you can find your project resources pulled off on to other work.

You sometimes find that silos are worse in functional teams than they are in project teams deliberately made up of cross-functional representatives. Individuals can be isolated, or make themselves isolated, and you have a job to do to ensure knowledge sharing and transfer within the team.

Finally, a challenge for functionally run projects is that they can suffer from lack of sponsorship and senior leadership. As the project is being run in the department, the leadership team may feel as if they don't need to appoint a specific sponsor for the initiative. That can cause problems when there are decisions to be made or when someone needs to take ultimate responsibility for the work that is being done.

Project

Project structures are those where the team is put together specifically to work on a project. This can mean taking people out of their day job on secondment for a fixed period. The team is made up of dedicated resources. You'll only find this on large projects where the workload means there is enough to do in a full-time role.

The main benefit of this is that there is no day job for the team members, so no conflict of interest back to their original team. As the project manager, you are ultimately in charge of the team and the people, so you have full authority over the way the project is managed. You can build a strong sense of project culture and create your own team identity.

It's an easier job to keep people focused on the goal and you'll often find people working on the team become passionate about delivery and keen to learn more about how to make the project a success.

Having said that, there are also disadvantages. The cost of a dedicated team can be prohibitive for all but the largest and most strategically significant projects. If you are pulling functional experts out of their day jobs to work on the project, they may find that they lose some of their core functional skills, making it harder to transition back to their normal roles once the project is completed. They may not even want to go back – and then you've got an issue with retaining hard-won organisational knowledge in the business.

The team can become inward-looking and isolated in outlook because they are solely focused on one project. If you tie up your best resources in this way it makes it hard to progress other projects at the same time because you might not have the skills you need in other people.

Finally, the project manager takes on a line management responsibility. Some project managers will love the opportunity to learn about line management and to develop this skill, as it can be an incredibly valuable experience. Some project managers will not want to be responsible for managing sickness absence, authorising holiday, processing expense claims and other such activities.

Matrix

Matrix structures are common in project-led environments. They are made up of individuals representing different departments and different areas of expertise so you end up with a project team that is truly cross-functional and cross-business. Individuals in the team might have responsibilities to several areas: one main line manager and then a 'dotted line' into another manager or the project manager.

This structure is so common because responsibilities at work, especially in small and fast-moving businesses, can't be linear and compartmentalised any longer. There are too many overlaps between professional roles. For example, someone with a 'digital marketing manager' job title might find themselves working within the marketing function, but with close ties to the sales team, the internal communications team to ensure the staff intranet is using the same brand assets as consumer-facing websites, and IT for all the digital back-end requirements. Companies organised along process lines or the customer journey will also find themselves running projects in a matrix environment.

If it sounds complicated, it can be, but being able to work in this environment is a core skill for a project manager. At the simplest level, your line manager might be the PMO manager, but your project sponsor could be someone in the finance team. That's a matrix structure where you have split responsibilities between your two leadership figures.

Matrix organisations can be an efficient way to use the company's resources. Subject matter experts can work on several projects at a time, and if you need someone from a different department they can easily slot into your team on a matrix basis. There's a lot of flexibility with how resources are deployed and it should mean that you can pick the best person for the job every time.

Matrix teams rely on consistent ways of working in order to be successful, so it's a good way to embed best practice. You can't have subject matter experts working on two projects and each project manager following a slightly different methodology. It would be too confusing, and it doesn't allow for standardised project reporting that allows for comparability between projects.

However, there are complexities of working like this, as you would expect. The major drawback is that conflict is common. Not the kind where people argue in the corridors (although that can happen too), but conflict between projects and their other responsibilities. Whose project takes priority when they both have upcoming deadlines? And what about the work the individual has to do for their line manager? It can be easy to make people feel overloaded and feel that they have to choose, whereas the project manager and their functional manager should be able to work together to identify clear priorities and schedules for the work.

Conflict can also appear in more subtle ways too, notably where functional managers ring-fence their best resources and refuse to let them work on projects. While in theory you should be able to secure the best person for the job, in reality you may not be able to get a particular individual to work on the team because of their other responsibilities and priorities. When you get a different person – perhaps someone with less experience or lower levels of skill – that can significantly impact your plans. You might need to train them (and that costs time and money). You might have to adapt your schedule because they don't work as quickly as a more experienced person. This can make for a difficult conversation with your project sponsor: all resources are not created equal in planning terms.

Generally, the advantages of matrix organisation structures outweigh the disadvantages for projects. Once you are aware of the challenges you can work to address them.

Although it's easy to pigeonhole organisations into running their projects in one of these three structures, bear in mind that organisations are more fluid than this in real life. In most workplaces there's a continuum of authority and structure on a project that looks more like Figure 3.1.

Figure 3.1 Organisational continuum for team structures

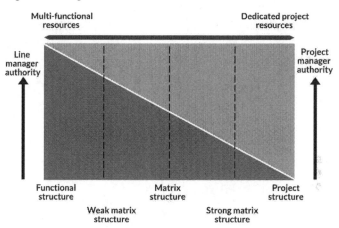

In structures where the line manager has the most authority over the resources and the project, the project manager has a less significant position in the team. Your negotiation skills become increasingly relevant as you look to secure resources. As you move further to the other end of the continuum, the project manager has more influence over the team and can adopt a more directive leadership style if that's appropriate for your workplace culture. Your project team will fall somewhere along this continuum and that will shape your role as project manager and the structure of the team.

IT departments come in all shapes and sizes, and so do IT projects. Here Sarah Johnson, Project Management Consultant, explains her experiences in two very different environments.

I was a programme director at a very small non-profit, though in all honesty my real job was being a project manager for our education, IT and marketing departments. In that role, and my previous non-profit project management role, I was largely self-taught through books, online forums and through taking PMI certification courses at a local university.

I simply didn't have anyone else I worked with who was from the project management field. My employers didn't provide any real structure around any of their projects and I was basically given full authority to decide how and when I put forth my new project management skills with no one knowing any better if I was actually doing the project management correctly or not! My typical day was split between doing operations for the non-profit and doing project management for various departments. Some projects spanned a few months; most of the projects were between one and two years in length.

Fast forward to my present job as a project management consultant where I'm based within an insurance company. My boss here has her PMP® along with many of the staff that I work with. Our Project Management Office has about eight dedicated project managers and business analysts building out a $15 million web portal for the company. There is structure, guidance, expectations and rules explained for how project management is done here and why it is done that way. It's basically the complete opposite of what I came from in many ways.

I like structure and being around fellow project managers that understand project management, so I really enjoy this position. And it doesn't hurt that I have better hours, benefits and pay than I had in the non-profit sector! My typical day here is 100 per cent project management with a sprinkling of admin work thrown in.

Sarah Johnson, USA, financial services

INTERFACE AND DEPENDENCIES

The role of project manager interacts with other roles in lots of ways. Some of these will be internal, such as your line manager, project sponsor, subject matter experts and others. Some will be external, such as suppliers, government agencies or regulatory bodies.

Common interfaces for a project manager are listed in Figure 3.2 and there's more detail on the important interfaces below, starting with the most important working relationship that a project manager has: that with the project sponsor.

Your most important relationship: the project sponsor

All projects should have a project sponsor, and this person is normally already in post by the time you are asked to manage the project.[8] If you are asked to manage a project and there isn't a project sponsor in post, you should seriously question the organisation's commitment to the project. While it might not be appropriate to refuse to work on it, you should certainly flag not having a sponsor as a major risk for the project.

The project sponsor is often a senior leader or director in the department which is going to be most affected by the project. You don't often (or ever) get to choose your project sponsor so you have to work with who you get. Here are seven things that your project sponsor should be doing for you to ensure the success of the project.

1. Securing resources

Securing resources is the first thing most project managers think of when they consider what a sponsor can do for them. That's because most of the project team members will come from the project sponsor's department – if they are the person who benefits most from the project then you would expect the subject matter experts to be based in their teams. That should make securing people for your project team relatively easy. If the sponsor believes it is an important project, he or she will jiggle around the work responsibilities and make it possible for the right people to have enough time to spend on the project.

However, there are also bound to be resources required that fall outside of the sponsor's team. These people might work

Figure 3.2 Core relationships for a project manager

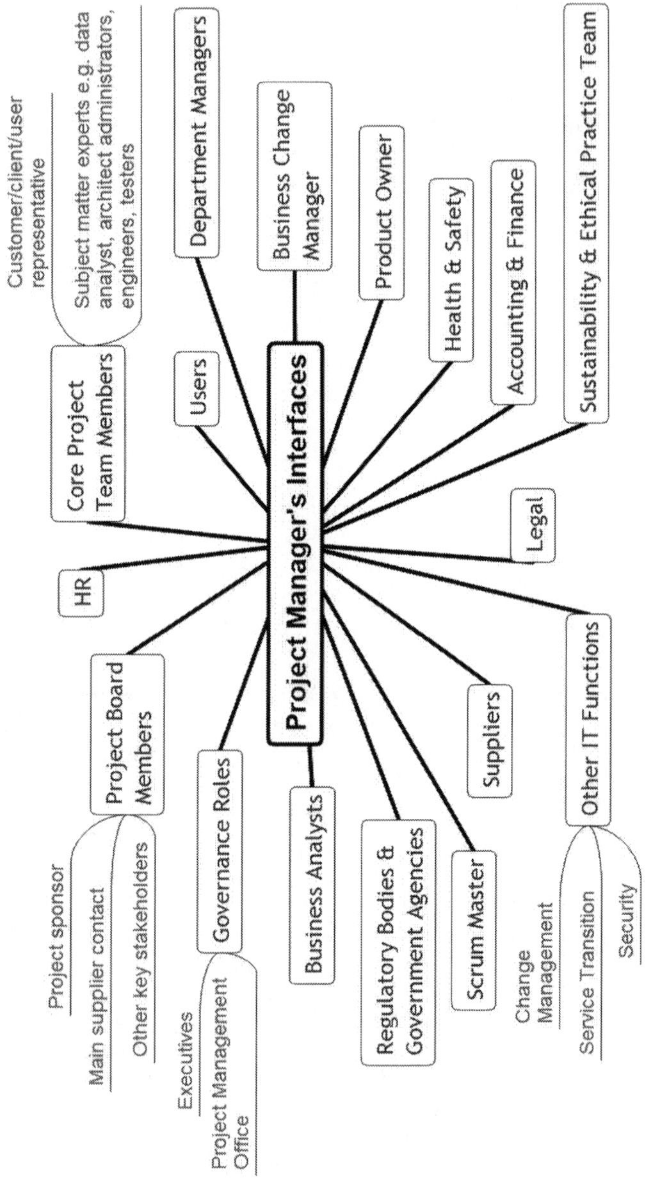

PROJECT STRUCTURES

for central services such as other areas of IT, HR, marketing or finance and this is where your project sponsor's negotiation skills come into play. The sponsor may rely on you to identify the kind of person you need on the team and for how long, and then they can go off armed with that information and talk to their peers about 'borrowing' that person for the project.

If your sponsor doesn't have the influence to get you the right people on the team then it's likely that your project will struggle. You may have to use your leadership and negotiation skills to talk to them honestly about asking someone else for help to secure the right resources.

2. Securing budget

Alongside securing people for the project team, the sponsor also has a critical role to play in securing the budget to manage your project. Again, if it is their budget that is funding the work, and they believe in the project, it should be relatively easy for them to put some of their cash aside for this initiative.

It gets harder when they need to rely on funding from other departments, which happens more often than you think. Despite it being all company money at the end of the day, there are often turf wars between departments trying to protect their own budgets. Project managers can get caught in the middle. You should be able to rely on your sponsor to sort out organisational politics and get you adequate funding.

Project sponsors are also important when it comes to budget and financial management. They are the people who approve additional spending, grant you authority to take money from the contingency fund or management reserves and they may have to authorise large invoices or purchase orders themselves.

If your sponsor doesn't have the authority to secure or approve funding, then your project will find it difficult to complete all the specified work: without the money you won't be able to get everything done. You'll need to talk to them about how to fund the work if they can't give you budgetary authority.

3. Approving change requests

One of the technical skills relating to project management practice is change control. This is a formal process for assessing any change requests, evaluating the impact on the project and putting forward a recommendation for whether the change should go ahead or not. This includes such information as how long it will take to do the work, the impact of this on the project plan, whether you have the resources to do it and how much it will cost.

This recommendation then goes to the project sponsor who will have the final say over whether the change should be incorporated into the project. It may involve them having to find additional funding or amending their expectations of when the work can be completed.

The decision about whether or not to go ahead with a change may be taken in a formal meeting such as the project board (more on the role of that group below) and may be discussed with the whole group before a decision is made. Or you may find yourself giving your sponsor an overview of the situation and what you would do if it was you while you are in the lunch queue together or waiting for the kettle to boil. Either way, the sponsor formally has the final say about whether a change is incorporated and they should feel comfortable making these decisions.

If your sponsor does not feel that they can act on (or reject) your recommendations when it comes to changes then you'll find nothing gets approved and the project does not move forward. Think about why this happens – it could be lack of confidence on their part or you might not be giving them the information they need to make a decision.

4. Communicating

Your project sponsor won't do all the communication on the project – a lot of that will fall to you in the role of project manager. But they should be communicating regularly to their peers, and upwards to their own managers. They should be explaining progress, getting help with any issues they cannot unstick themselves and generally championing the project.

Communication is important because it helps win over stakeholders who might be less than enthusiastic about the changes that the project is bringing in. It also raises the profile of the work which in turn helps with securing resources and budgets.

If your sponsor won't or can't communicate then your project will suffer from having a low profile. In turn that has an implication for the priority of your work and the amount of resources you receive to do the work. Talk to your sponsor about what you expect them to do in this area and provide the material to help them champion your project. They might not realise that this forms part of their brief.

5. Motivating the team

Another major part of project sponsorship is motivating the project team. That starts at the very beginning by setting appropriate goals for the project and explaining how the work of the team links back to achieving the strategic objectives of the company. They should be able to set a vision for the project and help everyone see how that will be achieved and what will be different once you reach your goals. They can use motivational stories and share customer experiences. In short, it's their job to create a positive environment where everyone knows what they should be doing and why. As the project manager, you can carry this on day to day, but the initial guidance should come from the sponsor.

Another way to keep the team morale high is to celebrate successes, and your sponsor can be involved in that too. Whether it is a quick thank you at the end of the week or stumping up the cash for a full-blown post-project party, celebrating success should definitely be on the agenda.

If your sponsor isn't interested in what the team is doing or in helping them achieve it then you may struggle to keep your team motivated during tough times on the project. You should feel as if you can turn to your sponsor for advice at any time.

6. Making decisions

Project managers need decisions made. You have a lot of responsibility in your role, bounded by the tolerances and sphere of control set at the beginning of the project, and you can make a lot of decisions alone. However, that responsibility does end somewhere and where it ends is where the sponsor's responsibility takes over. They should be able to make decisions that help you move the project forward, such as whether or not something should be in scope, what approach you take to dealing with an issue and how much risk they are prepared to accept.

Without such decisions, you'll be left either having to make them yourself which is really out of your area of authority, or you'll be stuck in a project that won't progress because no one will decide what should happen next.

If your project sponsor won't make decisions you are facing the very real possibility that your project will stop and ultimately fail. Think about why they are struggling to make decisions: are they missing critical information? Do they feel they need input from someone else? It could also be that they simply don't understand the consequences that failing to make a decision will have, and you should be in a position to explain that.

7. Managing risk

Finally, project sponsors should be managing risk. The day-to-day risk management process falls to you as the project manager, but the sponsor also has a critical role to play. They need to decide how much risk they are prepared to take on the project: too much risk and they put the investment in jeopardy. Too little risk and they restrict the project so much that the rewards become so little it's not worth doing the project at all.

Your project sponsor should let you know the sort of risk and the amount of risk that they are prepared to take – their personal risk tolerance and that of the company. This will help you manage the day-to-day risks appropriately and bring anything necessary to their attention.

A project sponsor who fails to understand risk management may end up creating more problems for the project, so if your sponsor doesn't seem to 'get' it, invite them to some risk management meetings and keep talking to them about it.

Project sponsors are essential people on the team, and great assets when they do what you need them to! Project sponsors who aren't engaged are difficult to work with and contribute to making the project harder than it really needs to be.

Project team members (subject matter experts)

'Project team members' is a very general term for the people working with you on the project, but it normally refers to the people who have a significant role to play in the project's successful completion. These are your core team: the people involved from start to finish and whom you couldn't do without.

The exact make up of this group is going to differ with every project but they are the experts who bring something unique to the team. They have the depth and breadth of knowledge required to complete the tasks and they'll have input into how the work is scheduled and done. Examples include:

- data analyst;
- system architect;
- database systems administrator;
- platform engineer;
- telephony engineer;
- network engineer;
- applications specialist;
- technical sales manager;
- development team member;
- software tester;
- scrum master.

You'll probably have at least one subject matter expert who represents the area of the business affected by the change, who is known as the 'Product Owner' in a Scrum team. This person can help define the requirements, explain how the project will affect their team and represent the 'customer'. The customer could be an internal department or an external group like a member of the public using your new app.

Subject matter experts can pitch in and help with so many areas of the project from testing to training and communicating back to their colleagues.

Department managers

Heads of department and team leaders are not people with a direct role to play on the project in that they don't do any of the tasks, but their staff are your project team members.

You'll have a relationship with them because you'll be working with them to secure the time you need from their staff. You'll also need to get them involved in setting priorities because they'll need to allow those people enough time to do their project work. If they consider the functional job to be more important, you will struggle to get their team members to commit to their project tasks.

Project governance roles

Within your project environment, certain roles have a governance function to play: these are all about monitoring and controlling the project's performance and ensuring it operates within the boundaries and policies set by the organisation. The governance roles typically are:

- **The project sponsor:** An individual with ultimate responsibility for the success of the project. It's normally the senior manager who holds the budget or resources and may receive the benefit of the project. For example, if you're delivering a new system for online invoice payment, the project sponsor would be a senior manager within the finance system with responsibility for accounts receivable, so their team would be using the system when it goes live. There's more on the role of the project sponsor and how to work effectively with them earlier in this chapter.

- **The project board:** A group of people who form the decision-making body on the project. This will include the project manager, the project sponsor (representing the users), the key supplier if you have a major contractor on the project, and other senior managers who hold particular influence over the resources, budget or success of the project. This group might also be called a 'steering group'.

- There may also be a level of **governance above the project board**. This is often formed of a sub-set of the executive directors and oversees the strategic implications of the project. The project manager may not attend these meetings; the project sponsor may represent the project. Whether or not you have a group like this will depend on the hierarchical make up of your organisation and the nature of your project. The more significant, complex or business critical your project, the more likely it is that you will have top level oversight in some form.

- **The project management office:** PMOs come in all shapes and sizes, and can play a governance function on your project. They also have a lot of names: yours might be called a programme office, an enterprise PMO or a project support office. Whatever the name, this team provides support to project managers and collects, consolidates and reports on project information. They are also the guardians of project management standards, templates, methodologies and tools within the organisation so you will find them heavily involved in process compliance. Your PMO may also be responsible for business assurance: making sure that the project remains viable and is on track to deliver the expected benefits, although your project board may carry out this role. PMOs can do a lot more than what's listed here, but they all have a function around ensuring projects succeed, and governance is a large part of that.

- **Quality assurance:** An individual or team with the responsibility for carrying out an independent check on what the project is delivering. The purpose is to assure the organisation that the outputs will be fit for purpose. Quality assurance is carried out by someone outside your project team and they may also look at whether you are following corporate guidelines or standards with regard to what you are delivering.

Business analyst

Whether your project is large or small, as a project manager you will no doubt find yourself working with a business analyst (BA) at some point in your career. A business analyst is a professional with great communication skills who can present complex ideas clearly. They are excellent problem solvers and can analyse difficult situations, and because of this they are an asset on project teams, especially in environments where constant change is the norm.

A business analyst on the project team will help you understand how the project contributes to the company overall and will ensure that you get a high-quality solution that works to achieve strategic and tactical objectives.

The role of a business analyst can vary, from someone who elicits user requirements to someone who contributes at a senior strategic level through portfolio work and assesses solutions before they become projects to ensure the organisation invests sensibly.

A BA has a role to play throughout the project but perhaps most importantly at the beginning. While the project manager is going through the project initiation process, the BA can be working in parallel defining the requirements. They understand the business circumstances that led to this project being kicked off in the first place and they can support the project throughout its life cycle. They can be the voice of the customer when the customer isn't present, and help translate the customer's requirements into a project scope that can be effectively delivered.

There's another key moment where working in tandem becomes even more important than normal: testing. The BA can track whether the requirements have been achieved adequately and advise the customer and project team during the testing phase.

As every organisation expects slightly different things from their BA teams, you will have to agree roles and responsibilities with the individuals.

If you have a business analyst on the project team, make sure that you include all the BA work in your schedule as some of it will have implications for when other tasks can start or when resources are available. Sit down with the BA and establish what their activities will involve, how much time they need to complete them and who they will have to work with. This will help you both avoid resource clashes or delays later.

The BA should attend all relevant project team meetings and be involved in project risk management. They have a deep understanding of the impact of the risk to the business and will also be able to identify risks that others on the team might not be able to see.

They can also get involved with lessons learned meetings as they will probably be the person on the team closest to the business users and with the best understanding of how the project is affecting the business teams.

Scrum Master

Agile is a commonly used approach for managing projects in a software environment, and is increasingly used outside of software development too. There's more about Agile project management methods in Chapter 4.

In an Agile environment you might be working with a Scrum team (known as the development team, which includes developers and testers) and a Scrum Master. Scrum is an Agile framework for getting work done. It describes an iterative way of releasing work, using small increments of shippable products. In other words, you drip out usable functionality instead of waiting for a 'big bang' launch at the end of the project.

Even if you are not part of the Scrum team, you may have to work alongside people working in this way and it helps to have a little background about what their roles consist of.

First, a Scrum Master is a specific role on a Scrum team, which is not the role of the project manager. They are not the owner of the product either (and we'll come on to Product Owners next). A Scrum Master helps the team use the Scrum tools and approaches effectively. They are supporting the team to use the processes in the best possible way to get the best possible outcomes.

A Scrum Master understands the values and techniques behind Scrum. They are subject matter experts in this domain and can support others in using the practices required. They support the Product Owner on the team too, by making sure that there is a list of requirements for them to prioritise, which is known in Scrum terms as the product backlog.

While the Scrum Master is primarily a coach and mentor to the team, they also have an organisational role to play on the team. They maintain the release plan and organise meetings. They facilitate conversations and keep the teams talking. They remove roadblocks and act in a way that maintains efficiency. The person in this role is constantly looking for ways to help the team learn what works so they can do more of that. It's a role that is responsible for the processes but not the people.

Product Owner

Product Owners are another core part of a Scrum team that you might come across on software development projects or through your work on other projects. It's not a project management role but it is complementary.

The Product Owner is a bit like the 'traditional' project sponsor. The person in this role is responsible for the project requirements and making sure that these are prioritised in a way that makes sense for the business. The requirements sit in what is known as a product backlog, and the Product Owner is responsible for setting and communicating the priorities related to these. The Product Owner has the business needs at heart and uses their business knowledge to ensure the project delivers something of value and strategic fit to the organisation.

The Product Owner is the main decision maker on an Agile project, and as Agile is a fast-moving environment, they could be called upon to make decisions frequently and in a timely fashion so that the project doesn't get held up. Project sponsors are often less hands-on than a Product Owner.

Project managers need a mix of skills. Below Aaron Porter, PMP and Certified Scrum Master, explains which he feels are the most relevant to IT project managers today.

For IT project managers working in a traditional environment the top two skills are: hard skill – effective scheduling and the ability to manage schedule dependencies between projects; and soft skill – the ability to tailor your communications to your audience; communicating both up and down the leadership pipeline.

For Agile project managers, the top skill is being able to manage effective retrospectives. This is probably less critical for an experienced Agile team, but ongoing improvement of team processes is critical. This allows you to evaluate what does and doesn't work, and to create and execute a plan to improve team processes.

Aaron Porter, USA, beauty and wellness industry

Users

As a project manager you'll also end up speaking to users. 'Users' is an unfriendly term for the people who are on the receiving end of whatever it is you are delivering as part of your project. If it's a new accounts payable system, it's the accounts payable clerks who deal with invoicing and client accounts. If it's barcoding technology for your warehouse, it's the pickers who use the handheld devices to scan boxes of products.

You may have a user representative on the project team – one of your subject matter experts. However, your project touches a group of users, not just that one individual, and they may come from a number of different teams or perhaps even be members of the public. As a project manager you'll come across the other users through your communication efforts, workshops, presentations, training and user acceptance testing (which will probably involve a number of individuals, not just the person who sits on the core project team as the user rep).

Users may make up your largest stakeholder group.

Business change manager

In some large organisations, change management is a specific discipline and you may find yourself working alongside a business change manager. The role of the business change manager is to integrate and embed into the organisation the change delivered by a project. This is very different from handling project change requests – for example, the request to add new features, which are handled within the project team using change control.

Business change managers (also known as business relationship managers) support and deliver change management in a business context. We can define this as the way we facilitate the shift from current practice to new practice in order to achieve a benefit.[9]

The change management role could be fulfilled by a team leader or functional expert. You might not have someone on the project team with that job title, but you should have someone focused on doing the work. In the absence of someone within the team doing change management, you can take on this role. Change management requires you to think about how the IT project is going to impact end users and what would help them get ready for whatever is about to be different. Change management tools include training, coaching, communication, readiness assessments and more.

Change management is implicit in the role of a project manager because it supports project success. The readier the people receiving the change, the more likely it is that it will stick and that the organisation will achieve the benefit it seeks.

External suppliers

Commonly, the external suppliers you use on a project are going to be third party vendors brought on to the project to manage an area of delivery where your own in-house team are not expert. This is often the case for packaged software deployment, where you buy a new system and the vendor's own team implements it in your business. Larger solutions, such as enterprise resource planning (ERP) products, have partner relationships with implementation firms. You don't get Oracle or SAP employees deploying their IT systems within your business, for example, but you would get certified partners who meet certain criteria and are experienced with the tools and what it takes to get them operational in a company.

Projects like this could involve a longer-term relationship with the supplier as they could be offering technical support and maintenance through an ongoing support contract, or you could include knowledge transfer tasks in the project plan so that your own team can manage the ongoing responsibilities of maintaining the software.

In these cases, the vendor will appoint an account manager or project manager to be your single point of contact into their resources. This is the person you'll meet with regularly to get an update on progress for their portions of the work and to discuss any risks, issues and anything else.

You may also have contract resources brought in on an individual basis, perhaps because you need an expert with this particular type of systems background for the duration of the project. Contractors are useful when you don't need that level of expertise in the business longer term, or when you just need an experienced extra pair of hands.

Some of your external suppliers could be companies with subject matter expertise, such as a legal counsel with particular depth of knowledge in an area of technical contract law, required before you embark on a new venture.

The role of the supplier on the project will differ depending on what you are hiring them to do. Their responsibilities will range from deploying technical solutions across your entire estate to advising on an element of accessible web design on a two-day engagement. They are providing a particular service or product required for the project's ultimate success.

Projects (even relatively small and simple ones) often have multiple suppliers. Managing multiple, overlapping vendors is part of your role as a project manager. Your objective will be to help them work together as a single team. While there are some commercially confidential details that you won't be able to share with them, it's easiest and most effective to think of the supplier project manager as an integral part of your project team and not someone 'on the outside'.

Regulatory bodies/government agencies

Another external stakeholder group to be aware of is regulatory bodies. These are groups that regulate your industry and practice. They set standards and policies, and enforce them, often with the weight of the law.

While not every project is going to have a regulatory or compliance element, there are plenty that will. For example, the EU's General Data Protection Regulation (GDPR) includes provision for reporting breaches to the relevant lead supervisory authority, so you could expect a project that was dealing with large quantities of personal data to want to be aware of what body that was and what, if any, additional requirements the regulations placed on the company.

Be aware of the regulatory bodies and government agencies that have a direct impact on your business and market, so you can ensure your project is compliant where it needs to be. There's an overlap here with your IT security or information governance teams.

If you are working in public sector projects, the role of government agencies becomes even more acute. Oversight for large UK public sector projects is carried out by the Infrastructure and Projects Authority, which is the government's centre of expertise for infrastructure and major projects.

Other roles

As each project is unique it's impossible to define the exact roles that your project will need. The explanations of the roles already discussed in this chapter are a good starting point for the major interfaces and relationships, but you'll quickly find that your project has implications for a wide range of other departments and roles.

Here are some other areas that your project might touch. These groups may be considered internal suppliers if they provide you with goods or services required for the project, or they may be subject matter experts for you to consult:

Health and safety: You may have to get input from health and safety managers within the business, depending on what your project is going to deliver.

Accounting and finance: Your project might need a dedicated capital expenditure, projects or overheads analyst if there are significant amounts of money being spent. If you have the opportunity to draw on expertise from the finance team for your project budget management, then do. It's one less thing you'll have to worry about and they are uniquely placed to help.

Legal: The role that expert counsel might play has already been mentioned briefly, but your own in-house legal team and data protection experts may also need to get involved.

Security: Many IT projects have huge data security implications, so you may find that you need to involve the information governance and security teams prior to designing your solution. They may also coordinate penetration testing (or other forms of 'ethical hacking') prior to signing off your solution as appropriate to move forward into delivery.

Sustainability and ethical practice: If your business has sustainability targets or ethical policies, you may find that your project needs to involve the guardians of these processes prior to design or delivery.

HR: Projects of all sizes affect the people in the organisation. Talk to your HR team early to understand any involvement they should have. They will be particularly helpful if your project involves hiring new people or making anyone redundant, and they can also advise you of any relevant unions which would need to be consulted prior to making any changes.

IT projects sometimes create additional businesses, or take over a service provided by another business, and in cases like these you would want to be aware of the Transfer of Undertakings (Protection of Employment) regulations (TUPE). Your HR team can advise if this applies, or if there are other aspects of employment law that you should be building into your project.

You might have any of these people on your core project team if you are expecting them to be heavily involved, but it's more likely that they will pop in and out of the project team as and when you require their input.

TOOLS FOR UNDERSTANDING YOUR PROJECT TEAM AND INTERFACES

There are a number of tools project managers use to keep on top of the seemingly never-ending set of working relationships on a project.

Project organisation charts

The most straightforward interfaces between a project manager and other roles in the business are codified in the project organisation chart. An example project organisation chart is given in Figure 3.3 showing a simple team structure.

There's a slightly more complicated project team structure in Figure 3.4, which has more people involved in a variety of roles. The interfaces between you and others in the organisation may look like this, or may look different depending on the project and your company structure.

Spend some time working out how best to display your project structure if it's complex. Your organisation chart might need to include external people (identified as such in some way). There might also be overlap between the roles. One individual can hold a number of roles, so if you've designed the chart in a role-based way you might have names on the chart more than once.

If you have space, your organisation chart can serve as a team directory if you include the contact details of each person.

Stakeholder register

The stakeholder register is a detailed list of the different individuals and groups who should be involved and engaged in the project. This is particularly important for IT projects. Often it's quite easy to think of the other technical teams who are affected by this change and it's possible to overlook the impact the work could have on other departments. The stakeholder register forces you to think through who else needs to know about your work.

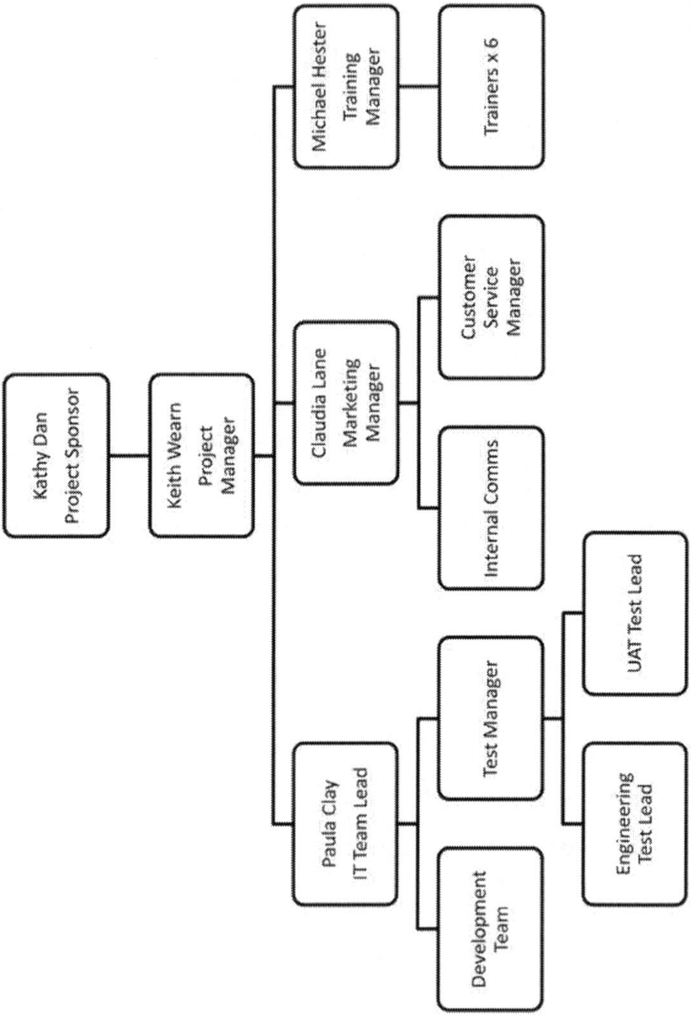

Figure 3.3 Straightforward project organisation chart

Figure 3.4 More complicated project organisation chart

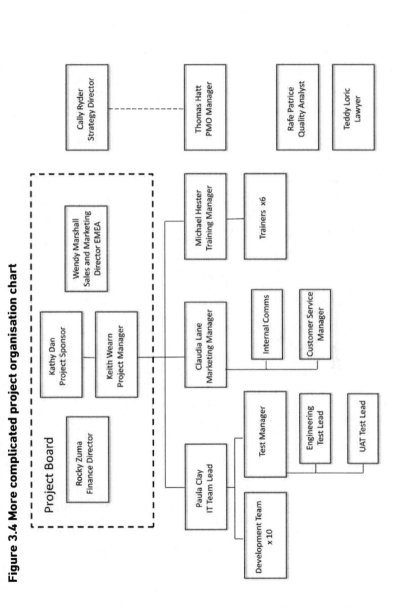

The stakeholder register includes names and contact information. More useful than that are two columns that you shouldn't overlook:

Expectations: This is where you can note down what each stakeholder is expecting from the project. What does success look like for them? Having this on your stakeholder register will prompt you to ask them the question. Then summarise the answer and record it on the template so you don't forget.

Influence: Categorise your stakeholders as 'supporter', 'neutral' or 'opposed' (or use other similar terms of your choice).

These two columns will provide useful information that will help shape how you interact with the individuals, teams and groups on the project. You can look for mismatched expectations that could lead to conflict. Knowing how influential your stakeholders are, and how they feel about the project (and note that this can change over time) will help you prioritise your time on engagement activities. You may want to spend more time with those who are not feeling positive so that you can convince them that the project is worth their time.

There is a lot of personal information included in a detailed stakeholder register, and that's fine if everything you write down about your stakeholders is positive. The moment you start labelling someone in the influence column as 'project denouncer; highly negative' or something like that, then you need to be *really* careful about who has sight of this document.

Use your professional judgement and if in doubt don't share it.

RACI matrix

A RACI matrix (pronounced 'racy') is a way of categorising stakeholders to define their roles and responsibilities on a project. Names (or roles, but names are better) go across the top. Tasks or project stages go down the side, as you can see in Table 3.1. Then you plot which person is involved in which activity.

Table 3.1 A sample RACI matrix

	Annie	Bill	Charly	Devi
Project planning	A	R	C	
Define requirements	C	R	R	C
Develop options	C	R	R	
Finalise solution	A	R	C	I
End user training	I	A		R

The RACI acronym stands for:

- **Responsible:** These people have responsibility for certain tasks. They are the 'creator' of the deliverable.

- **Accountable:** This is the person accountable for the job in hand who will give approval.

- **Consulted:** These people would like to know about the task and you would seek their opinions before a decision or action.

- **Informed:** This group gets one-way communication to keep them up-to-date with progress and other messages after a decision or action.

Put the right letter in the relevant box to show how that person is going to get involved with the project and note that individuals can fall into several categories.

You might also hear these charts referred to as a RASCI matrix (pronounced 'rasky'). These include an extra option to mark people as 'Supportive' (that's the 'S'). This is someone who can provide resources, information or will generally support you in getting the work done. Either is fine to use, and what you use may depend on your company standards.

Predominantly, RACI and RASCI are used as a roles and responsibilities matrix. They clarify the relationships between tasks and people on projects. It's a rookie mistake to assume that people always know what they are supposed to do. A chart that sets it out clearly like this explains what you are expecting of each person on the project.

Once you've created your chart[10] you can include it in your roles and responsibilities documentation for the project.

A RACI or RASCI chart is also useful for communications planning because it can give you ideas about which stakeholders need which type of communication at what points. It can flag which decisions are going to be made by consensus – this is definitely helpful to identify early on, because consensus decision making can be tough.

Another use for it is for process mapping. If you are going to change a process as part of your project you can use RACI to step through the process and record who is going to be affected by any process change. It's a really useful tool.

However, your chart isn't much help unless you keep it up to date as people do change roles and move into different positions of responsibility during a project, so when you are managing a project, make time to review it periodically.

Roles and responsibilities document

The roles and responsibilities document is very helpful, and should be put together in the early stages of the project. It's a formal way of setting out what each role is responsible for on a project team. As a minimum, this document includes the role title and a list of what that role needs to do on the project. It's also helpful, but not required, to include the names of people holding the roles. This can help the individuals focus on their particular responsibilities so that they can really own them.

You can add other information into the roles and responsibilities document including:

- authority and sign off levels per role;

- budget associated with that role;

- staff members reporting to that role;

- qualifications required to do the role;

- core skills and competencies required to do the role.

The organisation chart, the stakeholder register, the RACI matrix and the roles and responsibilities document combine to give you a detailed picture of the people who are required to make your project successful. You can find out where to get copies of templates for these documents in Appendix 3.

Mayte Mata-Sivera 'found' IT project management after studying chemical engineering. She describes how she built her skills in a new area below.

A lot of people ask me how I developed my career in IT after six hard years at Chemical Engineering School in Valencia, Spain. I'm one of those examples of coincidences in your life that help you to discover a career path that you really love.

A week before my graduation, one of the big 5 firms in the IT world reached out to me, offered me an internship plus free tuition for an SAP course. I struggled for days about accepting the offer, but I did take it in the end. I was not very tech savvy, but thanks to my mentors and coach in the company I learnt not only IT but also leadership skills that I continue to use and develop today.

After my experience in several IT organisations, I've realised that my passion is being a great project manager. There are some myths about project management. It's not just spending the day in front of the computer sending emails with due dates! It is also engagement, communication, leadership... I want to be one of those who really inspire the team, one of those who create more leaders.

> For developing some of my skills as project manager, I used not only my personal and professional network, but also social media platforms like LinkedIn and projectmanagement.com. They gave me the availability to choose the project that I wanted to lead, the group of people that I love to work with and to create a *team*. Also, using social media, I developed mentorship and coaching relationships with people around the world that helped me learn something new every day.
>
> *Mayte Mata-Sivera, USA, IT*

SUMMARY

In this chapter we looked at the role of the project manager within an IT organisation.

As this chapter explains, project managers work in a range of team structures. They work with a huge range of individuals: every team requires subject matter experts and support from different areas of the business and the project manager needs to be able to build working relationships with them all.

Read this

Emotional Intelligence for Project Managers (2nd Edition) by Anthony Mersino: A deep dive into the behaviours of successful project managers and how you can manage your own behaviour to drive better results in others.

Practical People Engagement by Patrick Mayfield: A book about leading change through the power of relationships. Excellent for people working in a matrix structure where you need successful working relationships in order to get anything done.

Do this

Find the organisation chart for a project or team you work on (or if you aren't working, find a sample chart online). Read through the different roles and check you understand what each does on the team.

Share this

Plan. Monitor. Control. Repeat #itpm

Stakeholder engagement: more effective than trying to manage stakeholders #itpm

4 HOW PROJECT MANAGERS WORK: TOOLS, METHODS AND TECHNIQUES

In this chapter we'll look at the ways project managers work. You'll learn about the major tools, methods and techniques used on the job day to day. The main distinction in working practice – although with more and more companies choosing best of breed and blended solutions it's becoming less distinct – is whether the project environment is Agile or waterfall/traditional. Understanding that terminology is the focus of the early part of this chapter.

We'll also look at the project life cycle, standards and methods and the core best practices and guidelines for managing projects including common processes. Finally, this chapter looks at the different types of software tools in use in project management and what you might find yourself using them for.

By the end of this chapter you'll understand the options available to you for doing the work of the project manager, although you will often find your organisation mandates some or all of how their projects should be managed.

AGILE VS. WATERFALL

In project management teams you'll generally find a split between people who manage their work with 'waterfall' (also known as 'traditional') project management and those who use Agile methods.

There is also a growing movement towards hybrid styles, where project teams use a blend of tools and approaches that best fit their organisation's culture, the skills of the team, the type of work involved and the needs of the project.

The approach(es) you'll use will be determined by the working style that best suits the team, the client, the business and the project and what you are working on.

Waterfall overview

At a high level, waterfall projects involve planning the work, doing the work and then delivering the work. The scope is rarely highly complex[11] and tends to have a great deal of certainty. This approach works well when you know exactly what the end result is going to look like and you can think of it as a series of linked and sometimes overlapping phases, that you can imagine look like a waterfall, as shown in Figure 4.1.

The flow of work in waterfall projects, especially those that relate to software design and delivery, is often graphically represented as a 'V' as shown in Figure 4.2. This makes it clear that each step at the beginning of the project can be validated and verified by a later step in the project. For example, the team accepting the end deliverable will validate it against the original specification to check it does what they were

Figure 4.1 Project life cycle represented as a waterfall

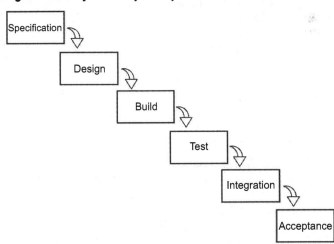

Figure 4.2 'V' model of delivery

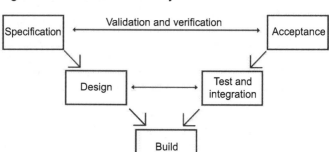

expecting. Testing is done by checking against the original high and low level design documentation, and so on.

The downside of the V model is that it doesn't easily include elements like project initiation, planning and closure. It's more aligned to the work that happens in the delivery and implementation phases.

The waterfall approach to managing projects can make it expensive to incorporate changes at a later date because that can result in a lot of rework. Because of this, there is an element of risk: it definitely helps to have user involvement all the way through and to ensure that what is being built is fit for purpose at every stage.

Agile overview

Agile project management is a term that encompasses various ways of getting work done that are incremental and iterative. Agile has its origins in software development and it's still highly associated with that kind of IT project. However, today teams in all kinds of industries and environments are embracing Agile tools and methods as a way to manage project work.

Agile comes in many flavours so even if you've worked in an Agile team for one company, at your next organisation things might be different. Scrum, Kanban and Scrumban are three

Agile approaches that are discussed in more detail later in the chapter. Extreme programming (XP) and Lean are other approaches that you will come across, and Agile project management draws on practices from these disciplines.

Teams can also be agile with a small 'a'. While agilists may debate the exact differences between big 'A' Agile and small 'a' agile, a simple way to think of the difference is that an 'Agile' approach refers to a specific, established method like Kanban or LeSS (Large Enterprise Scaled Scrum). Working in an 'agile' way is more about using the common, core attributes of these approaches: focusing on results, developing teams to work collaboratively and learning as we go. It's more of a mindset than a toolset.

All agile approaches have certain things in common:

- They have short, iterative development windows called iterations.

- Time and resources are fixed for an iteration; the functionality delivered can vary as the scope is prioritised for each timeboxed period.

- They have close working relationships between the development team and especially developers and end users.

- They reprioritise work regularly so that the important activities always get done first (and what is important can change daily depending on customer prioritisation).

- Teams have a nimble and flexible attitude which means they can quickly adapt to changing requirements and priorities as they happen.

Agile projects are more iterative than waterfall ones. Delivery is continuous, and new features are integrated with existing features on an ongoing basis. Features (known as products) are then released into the production environment weekly, fortnightly or on another regular schedule agreed by the team until goals the project wants to achieve have been completed. These tend to be projects with a high degree of scope uncertainty at the start: the team might not have any idea what the end result will look like.

THE CONE OF UNCERTAINTY

At the beginning of a project, the requirements might be a little vague, the exact nature of the solution might not be known, and other factors might introduce uncertainty too. This is normal – and more common than you might think. What this uncertainty leads to is a project with a large amount of unknowns at the beginning, and these are investigated as the project moves forward. As requirements are pinned down and assumptions unpicked, you get to know more about what is expected from the project. The uncertainty around the end result diminishes.

This phenomenon is known as the 'cone of uncertainty', which you can see in Figure 4.3. As you can see from the diagram, estimates are highly uncertain at the beginning. These are refined as the project team define more about the project, and at about 20–30 per cent of the time through the project (or phase, or iteration), the requirements and outputs become clearer.

The cone of uncertainty is an important consideration for project teams because making changes to software (or any deliverable) costs money and time. It costs more money and time the further through the project you are because typically it results in more rework. Making a change might absolutely be the right thing to do for the project, but everyone should understand that changes at a late stage in the project may result in having to spend more money to do those changes, along with the effort involved in testing it again and making sure the changes haven't broken anything else. Working in iterations is one way to combat these changes because you only have to focus on a small element of the overall scope at a time.

Being aware of and understanding variability in your project, assumptions and uncertainty will help you plan the work in the most cost-effective way.

Figure 4.3 The cone of uncertainty

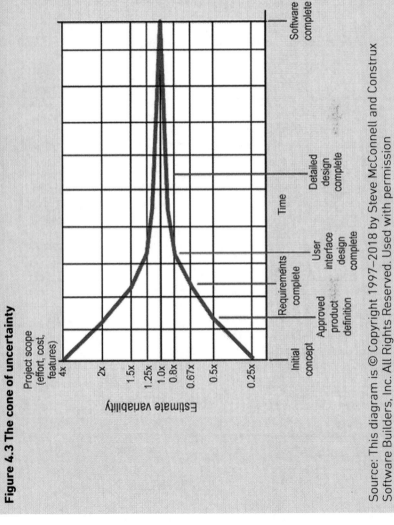

Which approach fits best?

Both Agile and waterfall approaches lend themselves to different types of project. A software project, where you can iteratively release new functionality, is a great fit for Agile tools and techniques. It's much harder to build a bridge in an Agile fashion, for example, but as that has a clear goal and may be something your company has done many times before, it's a perfect candidate for a waterfall delivery.

Traditionally run projects place the emphasis on scope – completing the bridge. The scope determines how long the project will take and how much it will cost. In agile projects, the emphasis is reversed: teams manage time and cost, and scope falls out of those. The constraints are around what you can deliver within the time and budget parameters for the team.

Ultimately, it doesn't matter much what approach you use as long as it works, and you'll find case studies of Agile in use across construction and engineering projects, traditionally run projects using tools commonly found in agile environments (with a small 'a'), agile teams using Gantt charts and planning over several months and so on. Today, we're seeing more and more overlap between the two – qualification schemes embracing both, like PRINCE2 Agile®, and organisations picking the best parts of a range of approaches to make a truly tailored way of delivering projects that suits their needs.

There are purists on both sides but as long as what you are doing is understood and embraced by the team and gets you the result you want in a structured way, you shouldn't get too hung up on whether the method you are using is 'right'.

When you start out in your career you'll be guided by the corporate culture you're going into anyway, and will adopt the approaches used by other people in the business managing projects.

Regardless of the approach you use, the project life cycle remains more or less the same.

THE PROJECT LIFE CYCLE

Earlier in the book, we saw that project work is different from the business of running a company, and one of the differences is that project work ends, while operational tasks keep going.

The project life cycle reflects this by setting out how project work happens and then how it stops happening.

Whether you're working in an agile or more traditional environment, your project will still have a life cycle so it's worth understanding the flow of activity. The jargon in use to describe the stages is likely to be different in your organisation, but you'll still be able to see how it fits together.

At its most simple, the life cycle has three main sections as you can see in Figure 4.4.

Figure 4.4 The project management life cycle

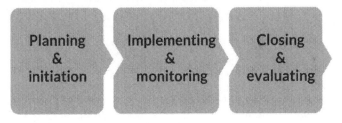

Planning and initiation

This is the beginning of the project, before any 'doing' work actually happens. It's where you establish what is required, get authority to start the work, get the right people involved and plan out together what you are going to do and when.

This stage can take a few hours of just you working by yourself, or involve several weeks or longer of onboarding and kick off. It all depends on the scale and complexity of the project.

Key points at this stage are to make sure you set clear, measurable objectives for the project. Without clarity, you won't know what you're trying to achieve or be able to measure the success of what you've done once you've stopped. You should also define the roles and responsibilities of the people who need to be involved so everyone knows what is expected of them.

What you end up with at the end of this stage is an approved plan of action for moving forward.

Implementing and monitoring

This is where the 'doing' happens – the activities that move you closer to having your result in place. If you are building software, it's coding and testing. If you're writing a technical manual, it's sitting down in front of a blank page and putting words on paper.

This is the longest stage in most projects. Waterfall projects may have several phases of delivery or implement solutions in a 'rolling waterfall' pattern. For example, rolling out new point of service sales systems to your branches might be done in phases: north-east branches in Phase 1, Scottish branches in Phase 2, East Anglia in Phase 3 and so on.

Agile projects will include multiple 'go live' points throughout the implementation stage as each iteration comes to an end and releases new functionality.

This stage includes the effort to check that you're moving in the right direction. This is the 'monitoring' part which involves regular points where you review your plans and compare what you said you would do to what you have actually done. If there are any discrepancies – say, for example, you are spending more money than you expected – then you make adjustments to what you are doing to bring the project back in line with your approved plans. In the case of spending too much, that would mean cutting back on spending, or if you can't do that, reforecasting your budget and asking for more money if necessary.

Closing and evaluation

The work is done; you've achieved what you set out to do. The project team is about to move on to other things.

But before you do that, you should wrap up your project carefully. A thoughtful close down makes it easier for other people to pick up and use what you have created, and to refer back to it in the future if they need to.

The closing stage involves completing a handover to the operational teams, preparing and delivering user guides, briefing the IT Service Desk on how to support the product and other tasks that make it possible for you to move on and for others to be responsible for ongoing support.

THE CHALLENGE OF HANDOVER

You've got to the end of the project: hurrah! But handing over your deliverables and products to the operational team isn't a task to be rushed. In fact, your handover should have started months before, as you should involve the operational teams, system admins and anyone else who has an ongoing part to play as soon as possible.

It's far easier to take delivery of a product if you know what is happening and what is coming your way. Talk to your operational counterparts and find out what they need and how they should be involved to make the transition into live service as smooth as possible.

The other essential element is evaluation. Many project teams build continuous evaluation into the way they manage work. After all, it isn't much help identifying at the end of the project that, if only you'd scheduled tasks with contingency, things would have gone much more smoothly. The first time that someone thinks, 'Contingency would have been helpful this week', you should be discussing that in team meetings and learning continuously, making improvements to the way you manage as you go. It's not good enough to only identify lessons learned: you also have to take action to get some value from them.

While it's better to build continuous improvement into your project and review lessons learned on a regular basis, it is also important to have an overall wrap-up at the end. Take time to assess what worked and what didn't on your project, and what could be done differently next time. This exercise helps the people involved to grow in their roles, and helps the organisation deliver more successfully next time.

Finally, this is the stage where you say thank you to your project team members and celebrate a job well done. You can, and should, be doing that throughout the project, but the final days are a time to remember what you have achieved together and make a point of recognising the sustained efforts of the team.

METHODS FOR DOING THE WORK

So how do you move through the project life cycle?

A method provides a complete framework for managing your project work and typically includes processes that help you monitor and control the work and tools (like templates or documents) to help you carry out the activities in a structured way.

PRINCE2® is a method for managing projects which is discussed in more detail in the next chapter.

You might also hear people refer to 'methodologies'. 'Methodology' tends to have a looser meaning, relating to the way your own team takes best practice as codified in your method or standard of choice and turns it into a set of processes, tools, techniques, templates, guidelines and so on that work within your organisation.

Let's take a look at some common Agile methods.

Agile approaches: Scrum, Kanban and Scrumban

All agile methods have the advantage of being close to the work at hand and enabling decisions to be made based on the reality of the project. They all rely on a close-knit team. There are a number of different agile software development methods including Agile Unified Process (AUP), Extreme Programming (XP) and Lean. In this section we'll look at three approaches: Scrum, Kanban and Scrumban, which is a method that blends the two. These are common approaches that lend themselves well to IT teams working on projects that go beyond software development.

Scrum

Scrum is a way of managing work within defined timescales called sprints. These generally last between one and four weeks and you work through your task list in that time. It's relatively formal in that respect, as deadlines are tightly respected and timeboxes do not change their duration unless the circumstances are exceptional.

Scrum, as the most widely used of these three Agile methods, has formal roles: Product Owner and Scrum Master. The team is also made up of other individuals from a variety of backgrounds who bring different skills to the team.

The Product Owner is rather like the project sponsor in a traditionally run project. She sets the vision and priorities. The main difference is that traditionally the sponsor is not part of the team day to day. Product Owners are right in there with everyone else.

The Scrum Master is the person whose role is similar to that of project manager: someone who leads and manages the Scrum process.

All agile methods need you to work out what has to be done (otherwise you couldn't get started). It's when you've got your requirements that the approaches start to differ. In Scrum, teams take their requirements from the product backlog. The Agile Alliance[12] defines the backlog as

> a list of features or technical tasks which the team maintains and which, at a given moment, are known to be necessary and sufficient to complete a project or a release.

You prioritise the work for each sprint during planning. There's a lot of negotiation at this point about making sure that the right tasks are being done in this planning cycle.

If a big task can't be done within the sprint timeframe then it will be split up into smaller chunks because the sprint dates absolutely have to be respected.

Scrum teams have strict processes to manage changes. Nothing new gets added during a sprint but it might make it into the next sprint.

Scrum has advantages for big projects that need to stay on top of the requirements and deliver regularly. The Scrum Alliance[13] says that the approach is particularly beneficial for complex projects.

Kanban

Think of the **Kanban** method as a way to visually manage 'To Do' lists. There are few formal constraints and you adapt your Kanban board – how the work is displayed – to reflect your workflow as you wish. You'll typically see columns for 'To Do', 'In Progress' and 'Done'. There are no hard deadlines but you can work towards a release or a larger goal.

Kanban is a far more relaxed method than Scrum. The team can add work when their task lists are empty or at any other point – as they don't work with iterations there are no fixed points where they have to come together to plan. As Kanban team members tend to have specialisms (instead of being multi-skilled individuals who can turn their hand to anything required), they can take their next task whenever they've finished their current workload and there isn't the requirement to wait until the next formal planning cycle to get more work allocated.

However, the team will respect the Work-in-Progress (WIP) limit. This limit restricts the number of tasks in the different stages of the workflow. For example, the team may decide they can only manage five 'in progress' activities at a time. The WIP limit means the team doesn't take on too much work and then fail to deliver anything. Limiting work in progress prevents bottlenecks and helps keep work churning through the team in a timely way.

You may not find Kanban in use in your project environment. It's less suited to formal project work and it's more aligned to operational teams dealing with a steady stream of work, although these might be thought of as smaller projects.

Scrumban

Scrumban is a blend of the Scrum and Kanban approaches as you'd expect from the name. The approach uses the idea of a continuous flow of work within longer planning cycles that tie in to your release dates.

There aren't formal roles prescribed for Kanban or Scrumban so you can use whatever you want, or no formal roles at all. Scrumban teams could be made up of specialists and generalists.

Scrumban teams do their planning when they run out of work to do, or in agile-speak 'when the backlog is complete'.

Scrumban gives you the benefits of timeboxing work into sprints and releases with the flexibility of being able to add new work and cope with business-as-usual type work too. That works well for teams who manage project work alongside keeping the business operational, which is the case for many IT departments.

DSDM®

There are a lot of different Agile methods in use and while Scrum and Kanban are common, it's also worth being aware of the Dynamic Systems Development Method (DSDM®)[14] from the Agile Business Consortium.

DSDM® is the longest established, full project Agile approach that draws together the flexibility of working in an agile way with an appropriate framework for project governance. That makes it a good choice for project-led teams, as Agile approaches can also be successfully used by operational teams (and Kanban in particular lends itself to that).

The philosophy behind DSDM® is that any project needs to be strategically aligned in order to deliver any real benefit. It's not dependent on any particular software or vendor solutions and it's a scalable approach to managing projects in IT and other business sectors.

Many of the tools and techniques available in the DSDM® environment will be familiar to users of other agile approaches including facilitated workshops, iterative development and timeboxing. However, there are many more team roles than in other Agile approaches.

DSDM® is an approach that can be used in conjunction with other project management approaches, enabling you to adapt traditional approaches and other agile approaches to work with DSDM® and cover the whole project life cycle.

BEST PRACTICE PROCEDURES AND PROCESSES

While there are some terminology differences between different project management approaches, there are some processes that are commonly recognised as best practice. The jargon your organisation (or preferred professional body) might use may well be different from what is set out below, but the concepts will be the same.

In this section we'll look at some of the main processes within project management that you'll come across time and time again. As this book isn't a 'how to do project management' guide, the processes are only covered at a high level, but you'll easily be able to find more detail on each of them in project management reference books. A couple of great ones with an IT bias are mentioned at the end of this chapter.

Requirements management process

The requirements management process elicits and assesses what stakeholders want from the project. There's an exercise to look for overlaps, spot anything missing and resolve any areas of conflict. Requirements are prioritised so that the 'nice to have' features are clearly identified – and the project team know where they should be spending their time.

Requirements in Agile approaches are managed through the product backlog: a list of prioritised features describing the functionality required at quite a high level. A lot of work goes into creating, maintaining and prioritising a backlog but once you've broken the work down like this it can feel like you've lost sight of the big picture. User story mapping is a different way of recording requirements that maintains the big picture. Requirements ('stories') are laid out on a timeline to create a map of the user's experience. While you'll still need to do some work to establish the detail for each stage, user story mapping is a straightforward way to visually represent what your project has set out to do.

Figure 4.5 shows a simple example user story map, for a project to build an app for managing employee expenses. In this case, the user's need is: 'As an employee, I want to manage my expenses from my phone, so that I save time dealing with receipts'.

Figure 4.5 Example user story map

Create expense	Take photo of receipt	Submit for approval	Check status
Open app on phone	Open camera app	Select manager	See claims in progress
Login	Take picture	Send for approval	See claims approved
Add description	Edit picture	Receive confirmation	
Add date	Attach picture		
Add cost code			

'As an employee, I want to manage my expenses from my phone so that I save time dealing with receipts'.

CASE STUDY: USER STORY MAPPING

Frances Place, Account Director at digital agency White October, explains how important it is to understand the project's vision and get this across to the team in a dynamic and meaningful way.

After years working on project teams, there's no doubt in my mind that a shared understanding and clear vision for the scope of a project, at the outset, is crucial.

I've worked on many projects with teams dutifully following lists of fixed requirements, only to discover we're going off in different directions because we've misunderstood the vision, or we've missed a detail because the requirements aren't exact enough.

Finding a technique that explains scope in the context of the vision is hard. Traditional project specifications do the job of detailing the scope, but they don't show how it all fits together. Requirements lists focus on what will be done and when, but not what it means for the user.

To fully understand the context of the project, and the user's point of view, the project team and stakeholders need additional briefing time, which often eats into precious delivery time.

And the specifications are fixed. There is no flexibility to change as the project progresses.

But what if there was a more dynamic way to capture changing requirements in the context of the vision that would brief and engage the whole team in the process?

USER STORY MAPPING: A SIMPLE WAY TO SCOPE PROJECTS

Agile consultant Jeff Patton was tackling the same issues. He needed to turn a list of requirements into something meaningful that communicates vision and shows the project priorities.

So he created user story mapping: a visual way to outline, sort and prioritise what you need to do.

The user story map shows the whole scope of the project in one place and is created through a collaborative process involving the development team, the Product Owner and any other interested stakeholders.

Patton's book, *User Story Mapping*,[15] gives detailed advice on how to use the technique for better project scoping, but in brief:

- Begin by detailing the tasks a user is aiming to achieve with the product, then group these into activities (high level goals) to form the backbone of the map.

- Have everyone in the team work together to add user stories as sticky notes underneath each task. These add the detail of what needs to be delivered.

- Involve the whole team in prioritising the user stories into versions which become the basis for the project plan.

The benefits of user story mapping

I have been using this technique for over a year and I now can't start a project without it – it is an invaluable tool for us for four reasons:

1. Seeing the product visually mapped out is powerful

As the features are told through a story on the wall in front of you, you can spot gaps and errors in your thinking before you begin to build the product.

For example, here you can spot whether you have captured stories for updating the user's profile but forgotten to add a requirement to create the profile in the first place. Errors like this are easy to spot when you tell the user's story.

2. Prioritisation becomes meaningful

There's something very different about the physical act of moving a sticky note above or below a release line from the virtual act of changing the priority level of a feature in a spreadsheet or online tool. It feels more real.

While it is the Product Owner who owns the prioritisation, the whole team sees the decision making. Anyone can challenge the choices made, allowing the whole team to push each other to deliver a viable solution with the least possible build work. This will get the product into the user's hands more quickly.

3. It allows you to adapt as you learn

The map is intended to be a living artefact that can be posted on your office wall, reminding everyone of the bigger picture of the product.

It can be used to continually review the backlog, adapting as you learn more about your users.

4. It is a tool for shared understanding

Perhaps the biggest, and most hidden, benefit is that of engagement. Having the whole team, including the Product Owner, together for a user story mapping session is by far the most efficient way of getting everyone to understand the product and each other. They are all part of shaping it, and become a stronger team in the process.

And, because everyone has contributed ideas to the map, they get a sense of ownership and are more invested in the project than they would be after a more traditional briefing.

I introduced a client to user story mapping. He'd been working on a project for over 18 months and had a clear vision in his head that he needed the whole team to capture and understand. When he saw the map he said, 'For the first time I can see the shape of the whole product in front of me'.

For him, his vision was finally becoming real.

Risk management process

Projects are inherently risky. Their unique nature means that you can't confidently predict the outcome. Add in the human element, and sometimes work becomes downright unpredictable.

A certain level of risk is acceptable on a project – and your project sponsor gets to determine that. Generally, the more innovative the project, the greater the risk it carries.

Project managers use the risk management process to track and react to risks. The risk management process involves these steps:

1. **Identify the risk.** Anyone on the team should be able tell you about new risks as and when they come to light.

2. **Analyse the risk.** Establish what impact the risk is going to have on your project if it happens. Risks can have a positive or negative impact. Example of a negative impact: If the cabling doesn't get delivered by Friday we'll have to postpone the installation. Example of a positive impact: If the marketing goes really well the website will get thousands more hits than we anticipated.

3. **Plan your next steps.** Once you know what impact a risk could have, you can plan to manage that. You might order cabling from a second vendor as a security measure. You might beef up the servers to capitalise on the extra hits you are hoping for. These actions offset the impact of the risk, giving you more control over it if it does happen.

4. **Monitor and repeat.** Monitor the situation with your risks and your risk management activities regularly so you minimise the chance that something is going to catch you off guard.

Risks are normally tracked in a risk register or log. This includes key information about the risk including:

- risk description;
- probability that the risk is going to happen (on a scale representing 'not likely to happen' to 'highly likely to happen');
- impact if it does happen (on a scale representing no impact to major impact);
- date raised;
- owner;
- risk response plan/next steps (how you are going to deal with the risk);
- risk status (for example, open/closed).

You can see a sample risk log in Table 4.1 and there is more information on how to get hold of project management templates to use on your own project in Appendix 3.

THE DIFFERENCE BETWEEN A RISK AND AN ISSUE

A risk is something that hasn't happened yet, but might happen.

An issue is something that has happened already.

A risk that materialises becomes an issue.

Issue management process

'Problem' has a distinct meaning in the IT community, especially in ITIL® environments,[16] but project issues are generally what most people would understand as a problem. They are something that has happened and that is affecting the likelihood of the project to deliver successfully.

Table 4.1 Risk log

Risk ID	Description	Probability	Impact	Owner	Response	Status	Date raised
001	Might not get the server components delivered in time	Likely	Moderate	John	Place order by Friday	Open	15 Jan

Examples would include:

- a supplier not being able to meet their contractual obligations;
- a key member of the development team leaving unexpectedly;
- an unforeseen bug in the system that you don't yet know how to fix.

Issues are tracked in a log or register in the same way as risks. For each issue record:

- issue description;
- owner;
- date raised;
- action plan (your response to the issue);
- date by which you want the issue to be resolved.

The action plan field is especially important because it explains what you are going to do about the problem. Depending on the scale of the issue and your proposed response to it, you might need someone else, such as your project sponsor, to sign off on your recommended course of action.

You can see a sample issue log in Table 4.2.

Change control process

Even on projects where the requirements are well-known, changes can happen. In fact, changes are more than likely to happen, so understanding how to deal with them is critical for a project manager.

Agile approaches can incorporate scope changes flexibly by updating the list of requirements, and priorities can change regularly according to business need. New requirements can be added into subsequent iterations without a major impact

Table 4.2 Issue log

Issue ID	Description	Impact	Owner	Response	Status	Date raised	Due raised
001	Networking supplier has gone out of business.	Major	Caroline	Emergency contract in place but isn't perfect for longer term. Work with procurement team on new tender; re-plan project to account for delay	Open	15 Jan	1 Feb for tender plans; 2 March for securing contract with new vendor

on current work. Because of the way development is done in a waterfall project, it can be harder to incorporate changes on the fly.

More traditional approaches use a change control process which:

- recognises the need for a change;
- assesses the impact of that change;
- recommends whether or not the change is made;
- incorporates the outcome of the decision that's made.

Changes can be highly beneficial for the project, especially if new information has come to light or you've just gathered some useful feedback on your new app, for example. However, if you're planning to change the existing scope that will most likely have an impact on the cost of your project overall and the time it's going to take to do the work. This is what you should assess so that the decision makers on your team can decide if the impact is worth the benefit.

These changes happen within the confines of the project environment, but when you come to release your IT project into production, you'll most likely have to go through a Change Advisory Board (CAB).

The CAB assesses the IT environment as a whole and manages all changes affecting the live environments. Your production changes need to be seen in context and will be prioritised alongside other standard and emergency changes that need to be done in the live environment.

If this doesn't happen, technical changes can layer on top of each other and have unforeseen consequences. For example, an engineer was replacing cabling in the floor of a data centre. On the other side of the racking, another engineer was working on something similar, but unconnected. The server stack ended up toppling over because the floor on each side had been weakened by the activity of the two engineers, who were coincidentally working on the same area at the same time. Having a change control process that looked at the environment as a whole would have prevented that from happening – that's what the CAB should do.

As an IT project manager, you should be aware of how the operational processes, like those run by the CAB, can impact on your project so that you can plan accordingly.

Configuration management process

Configuration management is the discipline of having control over who is doing what to what, and what version is the most current. It relates to creating, maintaining and managing changes to the products you are delivering. Configuration management and change control are linked: if you make a change, you'll likely have to update a product (known in this process as a configuration item) and record that through the configuration management process – often a configuration management database (CMDB). However, not everything on your project will be subject to configuration management.

Configuration management is common in coding teams where an individual can 'lock' an element of coding to work on so that their changes aren't compromised or overwritten by someone else accidentally working on the same area. You'll also see it in version controlled documents, which spell out the version history so you can check everyone on the team is working from the latest copy.

Using your project management and IT systems to manage the configuration of products is far easier than trying to keep on top of version control manually. How you are going to do configuration management is set out in your configuration management plan. Configuration approaches are often defined by the PMO for the business or department overall, so in your plan you could simply reference your team's configuration guidelines in a section in another document, such as your project initiation document.

Scheduling: Gantt charts

Where you have a high degree of confidence in the project scope and you know that your requirements are stable(ish), Gantt charts are a convenient way to display the project activities visually.

Gantt charts, named after Henry Gantt, the engineer who first made them popular, are horizontal bar graphs. Tasks are shown down the side. Duration is across the top. Tasks are plotted against the days and months where the work takes place, and there are normally columns for start and end date to make it easy to see the exact timescales for any given activity.

Gantt charts also have notation to show summary tasks, milestones and dependencies (which are how tasks link to each other). You can add columns to show the name of the person working on the task, percentage of work complete for a task and a multitude of other useful data.

Displaying your project schedule like this can give people an idea of the size and scale of the work, but it's common for stakeholders who don't work on many projects to struggle to read it. As a project manager, you may have to extract the key dates and create a summary timeline to use for communication purposes as well as having the detailed Gantt chart for managing your work.

A basic Gantt chart is shown in Figure 4.6.

Displaying work the Agile way: boards

Scrum, Kanban, Scrumban, DSDM® and other approaches use visual display boards. These show the tasks to be done and what stage they are in the process of getting done. You might hear them called Information Radiators, Kanban boards, team boards or Big Visible Charts (BVCs). The key is that they are readily on display and easily visible by the team. An example is shown in Figure 4.7.

Figure 4.6 Example Gantt chart

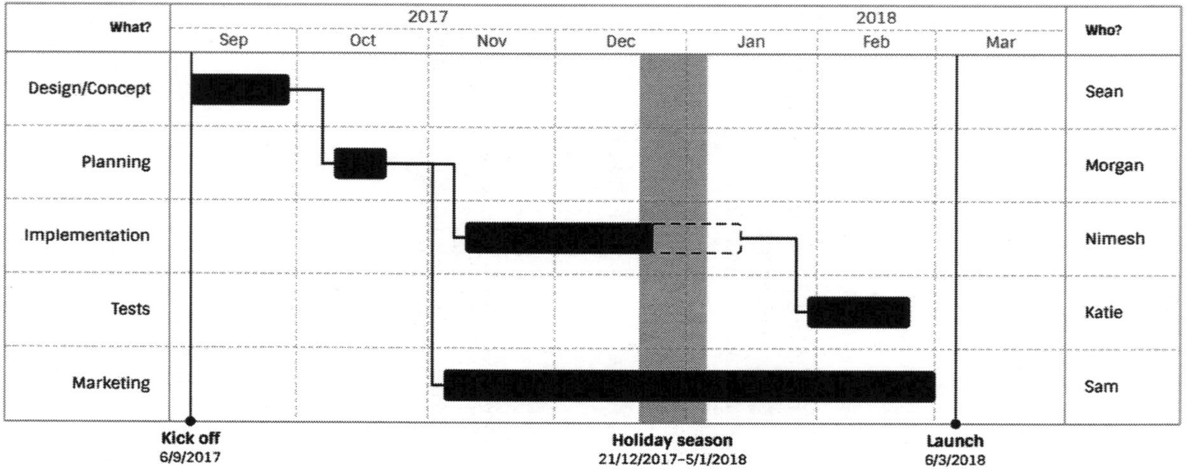

What?		Who?
Design/Concept		Sean
Planning		Morgan
Implementation		Nimesh
Tests		Katie
Marketing		Sam

Kick off
6/9/2017

Holiday season
21/12/2017–5/1/2018

Launch
6/3/2018

2017   2018

Sep Oct Nov Dec Jan Feb Mar

Figure 4.7 Example Kanban board From Cardsmith (cardsmith.co). Used with permission

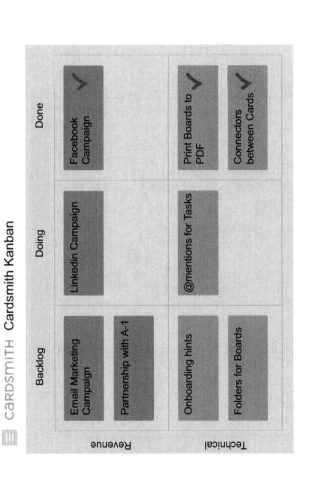

Teams using agile project management methodologies rely heavily on their board, but today that's just as likely to be a digital board as one on the wall of your office. While many agile teams are located together for ease of communication and efficiency, more and more agile projects are run with remote teams, and Agile project management tools have grown to adapt to that.

Work moves visually between columns. It's a really simple communication tool for teams and shows progress clearly.

Kanban boards and Scrumban boards remain in play for the duration of the project. Both of those approaches rely on a continuous flow of work, so the tasks are added on one side of the board and make their way over to the other side where they then represent completed activities until they are removed.

Scrum task boards are wiped and reset every time a new sprint starts, to reflect the requirements planned for the new sprint. Scrum boards also have other differences, such as the fact the backlog tasks are described as user stories. User stories are explained in the case study from Frances earlier in this chapter.

Both Kanban and Scrumban have a 'work in progress' limit. For example, perhaps a developer can't deliver more than one feature at a time, so his or her workload would only show one at a time.

Measuring progress: burn-down and cycle time charts

A burn-down chart is the key way to measure progress in Scrum. Burn-down charts show you how much work you have 'burned down', i.e. completed.[17] They illustrate how much work is still to do and what the ideal progress would be. This is similar to the calculations of actual work vs. planned work that you can derive from a Gantt chart.

Burn-down charts also display other performance metrics such as the concept of 'value'. The value line on the chart should go up as the team completes more work.

This sounds complicated but once you know how to read a burn-down chart like the one shown in Figure 4.8 they are simple and visual ways to display project progress.

Progress on Kanban projects is measured in two ways: cumulative flow – a graph that shows total items in progress; and cycle time – a measurement that shows how much time it takes to complete one task.

Scrumban uses cycle time too. A sample cycle time chart is shown in Figure 4.9.

Measuring progress: earned value

The waterfall (or traditional) way of measuring progress is also through using a graph to show work completed over time, but it's a technique called earned value management. The expected performance baseline is compared with actual performance and budget, providing an integrated view of how the project is doing in both expenditure and schedule against what was expected.

Earned value is a useful project management technique but it's often considered 'advanced' and it is not in use everywhere. Plotting actual performance against your schedule baseline and calculating if you are ahead or behind your plan is a simpler way to measure progress (plus your Gantt chart software will often do this for you).

Resource management and scheduling

All projects use 'resources', which is a term that refers to physical assets like cabling, monitors and office space but also – and more commonly – refers to people. People need to be allocated to the appropriate tasks in a way that doesn't

Figure 4.8 A burn-down chart From Eylean (eylean.com). Used with permission

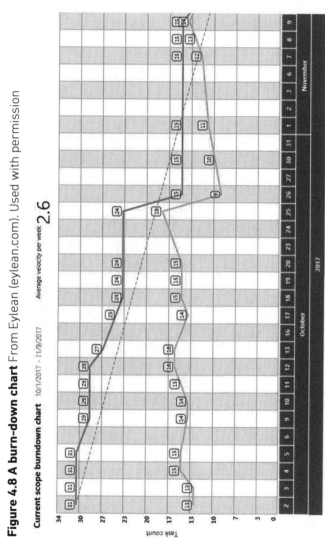

Figure 4.9 Cycle time chart From Eylean (eylean.com). Used with permission

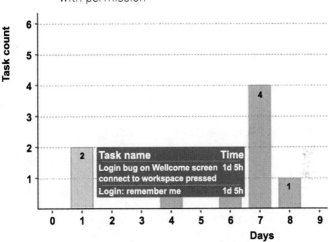

overload them but equally doesn't end up with them sitting around waiting for work to come in.

Resource management is the discipline of making sure the right people are working on the right tasks. In self-managed teams, individuals can choose their own next priority task. In other project cultures, it's common for the team leader or project manager to work with the individuals on the team to assign tasks to the person best suited to do them, so it's important to know the strengths and weaknesses of your colleagues.

The project initiation document (also known as the PID) sets out the list of core skills required to complete the project work and will often include a list of resources.

Stakeholder management

Stakeholder management is the process of identifying, analysing and planning the work to do with how you are going to engage people on the project. It includes developing a stakeholder management plan which starts with a stakeholder register and a RACI matrix.

As well as organising the right people to work on the project, you also have to keep the team and wider stakeholder group engaged. There's more on stakeholder management and engaging the team in Chapter 3 – being able to effectively work with stakeholders is a core best practice.

WHAT IS STAKEHOLDER ENGAGEMENT?

Stakeholder engagement is distinct from stakeholder management. In project management books of yesteryear you won't read much about engagement. The term has developed with a distinct shift in project management jargon to reflect the fact that you can't *manage* people's reactions or behaviours. It's arrogant to think that you can, so reframing the language related to the tasks involved in working with stakeholders can help you see the activities in a different way.

Thinking about 'engaging' people instead of 'managing' people can help you be more open to the idea of working together, inspiring commitment and being part of a wider team.

Governance and reporting

Whatever approach you use, you're going to have to periodically report to someone (normally your project sponsor) about the progress you are making. There's also some level of governance that you'll have to apply to make sure that you are on the right track.

Governance is the oversight applied to the project by the project manager, project board and other executives or groups such as the PMO to ensure that the project is being managed effectively and is still on track to achieve the expected benefits.

Project reports come in various formats, from online dashboards built into your software to spreadsheets, tables or a simple email with a list of progress – they don't have to be complicated.

Appendix 3 has more information on how you can download sample report templates to use in your own project, or you can talk to your PMO about what they expect to see. The most important thing is that you are reporting the information that your project sponsor wants to know about.

Financial management and cost control

Your project budget needs careful management, so project management best practices include financial management and cost control.

This is all about ensuring that you are spending the right amount of money on the right things and you are accurately forecasting your budgetary needs. The control elements look at whether you are on track and the impact on cash flow of your planned project expenditure.

Cost tracking may either be built into your project management software or carried out in another tool such as a spreadsheet. Figure 4.10 shows an example of project cost items, budgeted cost, actual cost and variance to budget. This tracking allows the project manager and business team to keep track of where the money is going.

Project scheduling software often allows you to track costs associated with a particular task, especially if you are billing for resource hours and keeping precise track of how long work is taking so you can charge for it.

Figure 4.10 Example project budget tracker

Budget Tracker

Item	Budgeted Amount	Actual Amount	Variance
Infrastructure			
Server	£ 9,000	£ 8,995	£ 5
Switch	£ 15,000	£ 14,750	£ 250
Cabling	£ 3,500	£ 3,750	-£ 250
Installation	£ 6,750	£ 7,725	-£ 975
Total Infrastructure	£ 34,250	£ 35,220	-£ 970
Development & Testing			
Software package 1	£ 30,000	£ 31,250	-£ 1,250
Software package 2	£ 35,000	£ 34,800	£ 200
Testing Phase 1	£ 6,500	£ 6,500	£ -
Testing Phase 2	£ 6,500	£ 6,500	£ -
Penetration Testing	£ 13,750	£ 13,700	£ 50
Total Development	£ 91,750	£ 92,750	-£ 1,000
Contingency	£ 5,000	£ 2,600	
Contingency	£ 5,000	£ 2,600	£ 2,400
Totals:	**£ 131,000**	**£ 130,570**	**£ 430**

Quality management

Quality management is a process that ensures the final deliverables from the project are of an appropriate quality. You write a quality plan at the start of the project that sets the standard for the quality you wish to see at the end. The plan specifies how you will 'do' quality – what policies, procedures and guidelines the team will follow to ensure a high-quality outcome. You can also set specific quality targets or metrics for deliverables.

Quality management processes enable you and the team to check that you are on track to achieve those targets and specify how you will know if you have achieved the quality you set out to – perhaps, for example, through peer reviews of lines of code.

SOFTWARE TOOLS

The market for project management software tools is huge. The most recent Gartner Magic Quadrant on software tools will show you the current key market players.[18] Typical project management software tools fall into these categories:

- collaboration tools;
- task management tools;
- enterprise project management tools;
- Agile tools.

Collaboration tools

Collaboration tools are designed for teams to work together wherever they are based. While they have a distinct use for virtual teams who are not located in the same office, even teams who are based together have adopted these systems to make it easier to store information, work remotely when they have to and chat more easily.

It's highly likely that in your work as a project manager you'll be expected to use collaboration tools. Research shows that 94 per cent of project managers use collaboration tools on their projects.[19] The most common reason cited for using collaboration tools is document sharing: 27 per cent said they used their tools for this.

Communication was the second most common reason, with over one in five respondents saying they used it for that. The third most common response was working with internal stakeholders, which accounted for 20 per cent of the responses.

Other reasons for using collaboration tools included:

- To schedule or assign work: 17 per cent of respondents.
- To work with external stakeholders: 11 per cent of respondents.

- For other reasons: 3 per cent of respondents. This figure is made up of using the tool as a knowledge base, for lessons learned, transparency, audit trails and version control among other reasons.

Examples: Microsoft SharePoint, Skype, Slack, Yammer and Huddle.

Task management tools

When you don't need the full functionality of an enterprise-grade project management tool, an app aimed at helping you manage tasks with your team might be all you require.

These systems are generally cloud-based, subscription services that manage a task list. They are suitable for smaller projects or informal environments.

Examples: Asana, Apollo and Whiteboard.

Enterprise project management tools

These systems cover the major functionality required to run a project in a non-Agile environment. They offer enterprise-grade approaches to managing projects, often with modular add-ons that allow you to manage beyond the project life cycle, for example, by managing bugs or feature requests, offering helpdesk functionality or work management.

They also often offer the ability for teams to 'roll up' projects and see the entire portfolio of work in a single view or dashboard. This can be useful for the leadership team and the Project Management Office, as having this single view of all ongoing project work can help inform decisions about what new projects should be approved and where there are likely to be gaps or pinch points in resourcing.

Typical project management features to look out for – the ones you would use day-to-day when running a project – include:

- Gantt charts including baselines and automatic calculation of the critical path;
- timesheets;
- resource allocation;
- risk and issue management, change control and tracking;
- dashboards and reporting;
- cost, budgeting and expense management.

They may also have some collaboration features to enable remote teams to work on the same projects and documentation.

Many tools that fit into this category are available either as on-premise local installations or Software as a Service models.

Examples: Microsoft Project, TeamworkProjects, Celoxis, ProjectManager.com, LiquidPlanner, Podio, Genius Project, Primavera, Planview and OpenProject.

Agile tools

These software products support Agile methods by providing boards on screen instead of on the wall.

Examples: Cardsmith, Trello, Eylean and Asana. Some tools that started out targeting traditionally run projects also have the option to display tasks on a board – for example, ITM Platform.

There are hundreds of software products marketed at project teams. Your company will probably have one already so you will find yourself using what is already installed. Go through any walkthrough or introduction built into the software and use the help files to get started. Most of the products are self-explanatory but the more advanced products such as Microsoft Project and Primavera may require training to help you get the best out of them. There are video tutorials for most products available on YouTube, either created by the vendors or by enthusiastic users.

SUMMARY

Agile and waterfall/traditional approaches are different ways of managing projects, suited to different environments and deliverables. There's more and more awareness and take up of blended solutions that offer the best of both in a tailored way.

The project management life cycle is the way you get from an idea through to the completion of the delivery work and on to project closure.

There is a range of best practice processes and techniques which enable you to manage your project effectively including requirements management, change control, risk and issue management, resource management, stakeholder engagement, governance, reporting, quality management, configuration management and scheduling.

Software tools are used for collaboration, task management and the full range of project management activities in both Agile and non-Agile environments.

Watch this

A short video on the roots of DSDM® and the Agile Alliance: vimeo.com/99321882

Read this

There are hundreds of books that will teach you the fundamentals of doing project management and expound upon the processes and guidelines mentioned above. These are definitely worth the investment:

- *Agile Foundations* by Peter Measey: this book provides a comprehensive introduction to Agile principles and methodologies and is the official textbook for the BCS Foundation Certificate in Agile.

- *Growing Software* by Louis Testa: a book about the processes and approaches required for software delivery teams to deliver projects successfully – also useful for other IT practitioners.

- *Making Things Happen* by Scott Berkun: this book is an honest and funny look at what it takes to manage projects, from someone who worked at Microsoft for nine years. Another good solid reference guide to the project management life cycle and core processes.

- *User Story Mapping* by Jeff Patton: referenced earlier in this chapter, it's an overview of using this tool on projects.

- *Succeeding with Agile: Software Development Using Scrum* by Mike Cohn: this is an actionable guide to getting started with Agile and includes lots of case studies.

- *Essential Scrum* by Kenneth Rubin: this book provides a comprehensive guide to Scrum.

Take it further

There is a concept particularly prevalent in Agile communities called DevOps, and while that is outside the scope of this book, it's worth looking into if you work in an Agile environment.

Share this

My project management tool of choice is ... #itpm

I'm using #pm best practices #itpm

Agile, traditional or both? What do you use as an #itpm?

5 CAREER PROGRESSION AND RELATED ROLES

Project management is a large field and there are plenty of opportunities for developing a long-term, successful career within the discipline.

In this chapter we'll look at:

- How to get into IT project management: finding your first role.

- How to get on in project management: adding qualifications to your CV to show your expertise.

- How to move on in project management: programme management roles and other opportunities for taking the next step after project management.

- How to move out of IT project management: what options there are for leaving a project delivery role and how your project management skills can support you on other career paths.

By the end of this chapter you'll understand a typical route for career progression and the qualifications that will support your career journey.

GETTING INTO PROJECT MANAGEMENT

The projects that you read about in the media are often high profile, with budgets in the multi-millions or even billions. They all seem to be led by highly experienced project managers who have the confidence and skills to deal with the complex sociopolitical environments of their projects, international and virtual teams and other factors that make their work particularly challenging.

When faced with that view of projects, you might wonder how people ever got started. But all those high-profile leaders got started in the same way that you can: managing smaller initiatives, practising their core skills and learning through training and on the job.

You can also build up your experience at home: if you are keen to learn the principles and tools, why not have a go with products like Microsoft Project, Trello or Asana to make a simple project plan for decorating a room or planning an overhaul in the garden, for example? Similarly, you can also use project management approaches in your current role – even if that is nothing to do with project management. Look for opportunities to manage work in a structured way and use project management principles to support that.

These are good ways to build up something to talk about at interview and to show an employer that you are interested in project management as a career, while you work on securing a role.

If you talk to project managers or read through the stories in this book you'll realise that there are as many ways to build a career in the field as there are people. However, there are three common ways of entering the job market in a project delivery role:

- through higher education;
- through an apprenticeship;
- through direct entry.

Higher education

There are lots of undergraduate degrees and postgraduate certificates and degrees with a project management concentration. Whether you opt for a module of project management within a degree in a different discipline, or take one with a high proportion of project management is up to you and will depend on the direction you see your career taking.

A project management individual module is definitely worth considering because even if you don't end up in a 'full' project management role, you can guarantee that most jobs these days will require you to be able to plan and organise your own work and possibly the work of other people as well.

Majoring in project management or taking a combined degree could also give you a professional qualification (or the background and education required to be able to sit the exam for a professional qualification). That's a way to round out your education so it's worth considering if your chosen degree course will count in any way towards industry qualifications.

Apprenticeships

An apprentice is an employee whose company receives funding to train them and to put them through professional assessments. It's on the job training with support for structured learning too, and it's a great way to get into project management with little previous practical experience.

At the time of writing, higher level project management apprenticeships in the UK are evolving. The Associate Project Management Apprenticeship Standard (APM) – also at level 4 in the Regulated Qualifications Framework from Ofqual, which equates to the first year of higher education – is a Trailblazer apprenticeship and has been available since January 2017, but only to candidates from England.

The Trailblazer apprenticeship is the new standard and has been developed by an employer group specifically to meet the requirements of a particular profession. APM is involved with the project management apprenticeship standard and the two-year scheme includes taking the APM Project Management Qualification (PMQ).

Over your time as an apprentice you'll develop the skills and behaviours required to succeed in the job, and these are assessed during a presentation and discussion-format interview at the end of your apprenticeship.

Degree-level apprenticeships are being developed as well.

The Higher Apprenticeship in Project Management at level 4 is available in Scotland and Wales. This also includes a professional qualification, the EAL[20] Level 4 Diploma in Project Management.

Direct entry

You can't walk into managing a multi-million pound project, but there are plenty of entry level IT jobs that will give you the experience you need to work up to that.

Look for jobs advertised as project coordinators, project office assistants or junior or trainee project management roles within technical functions. These are all involved in the discipline of managing projects, and with some experience you'll be able to move into managing larger projects by yourself.

Project coordinator, or a role with a similar title that has the objective of assisting a project manager or team of project managers, is a very good entry point, so let's look at that in a bit more detail.

The role: Working on larger projects in a support position to assist with whatever the project manager, wider team and senior management need. This could range from being in charge of updating documentation, making travel plans, organising meetings and taking minutes, calling team members to gather status reports, managing the project management software tools for the team and anything else. It's a hugely varied job.

The projects: These will vary depending on your industry and the company and team you work within. You may be able to manage smaller projects on your own in this role, especially if they are initiatives the business does regularly, such as updating a system, where there is a defined project plan and the work is low risk.

Watch out for: Being a general dogsbody. There's a lot of admin in project management and much of it can be offloaded onto the project coordinator. However, that shouldn't mean you get all the horrible jobs. A good employer will ensure that you have the opportunity to work-shadow experienced project managers and be exposed to different areas of the team to ensure you are growing your skills. A not-so-good employer could end up treating you as a glorified secretary. That's not what project management is all about.

Tips for your first role

Whatever your route into project management, you're going to want to make a good first impression. Here are five tips for making your first few weeks in a new entry level job as a project coordinator go smoothly, although many of the tips will still apply if you are going directly into a project manager role.

1. Meet the team

Make time to meet your direct colleagues, people doing a similar project delivery role to you (the other project coordinators, if there are any) and your project team. Schedule one-to-one meetings with key people like your project manager and project sponsor so that you can find out more about what you will be doing for them and how your work supports the team as a whole.

The people you are working with day to day might not have been involved in your recruitment, so be prepared to talk a little about your background and experiences to date too.

2. Find your project context

In other words: how does your project fit into the bigger picture? Your direct line manager or project manager should be able to tell you this. It's a huge help for prioritising work and understanding why decisions are made – if you understand how your project ties in with other large initiatives you'll suddenly find that conversations that felt random make a lot more sense.

It's also better for you because you can more easily explain the value of your work to other people if you understand how what you are doing contributes to the business goals overall.

3. Clarify your objectives

Understanding the project context is helpful for the big picture, but what about the work you are responsible for? You also need to understand your personal objectives and how the company will rate your contribution.

This is normally clear on a structured scheme like a higher apprenticeship, but if you've entered the workplace after higher education or directly with no previous qualifications, you'll have to sit down with your manager and set objectives for the year.

Don't be scared to do this – all employees have targets, goals and objectives as a way to monitor performance and support development, so it's a normal part of your conversations with your manager.

4. Learn the tools and processes

Prioritise learning as much as you can about the methods, approaches and tools in use in your team. Find out how you can access the library of project management templates if there is one. How should you be reporting and recording your progress?

Get logins to all the IT tools you need and watch how other people use the processes. Ask questions, take notes and learn. The first three months at a new job are the perfect time to absorb a lot about the company and team culture and how work gets done.

5. Smile!

You worked hard to get this break into IT project management, and hopefully you'll be in the field for a long time. However nervous you feel meeting new people or doing new tasks, try to be polite and positive. You don't need to be best friends with the people at work, but you'll go further in your career if you are personable and helpful because people will enjoy working with you.

MOVING ON IN PROJECT MANAGEMENT

Having secured a project management role, your natural career steps will be to take on larger and more complex projects.

The other important thing for individuals looking to solidify their position as a career IT project manager is to consider the importance of qualifications. A qualification can demonstrate to employers that you are serious about your career path, and that you know what you are talking about. Plus the effort of studying for an exam shows that you are committed to continuous professional development (CPD). And you might learn something.

There are a number of project management qualifications that you can go for. Below we'll look at the most common options that reflect the major methods and standards in place that are recognised by most UK employers.

There are lots of different ways that people gain their qualifications. Below project manager Donna Unitt explains how she gained hers.

I was a super user at my company and then moved into an IT project management role. I took my APMP [now PMQ] qualification which definitely helped me manage projects. I also took the PRINCE2® Practitioner qualification which was good to have as it is widely recognised and has a solid methodology, but I use those concepts less in my day job today.

Once I was in an IT project management job and had gained my project management qualifications I then went on to do a Master's in Technology Management. Put like that, it sounds like I did them the wrong way round but that path made the most sense for my career! My degree helped me understand how systems and infrastructure fit together.

I've recently done a change management course as well.

Donna Unitt, UK, supply chain consultancy

CAPM®

The Certified Associate in Project Management (CAPM)® is the introductory level credential from PMI. It's designed to demonstrate your understanding of the fundamental knowledge, terminology and processes of effective project management. It's globally recognised and it's not essential to have any experience of managing a project before undertaking it so it's perfect if you are starting out in your first project role.

However, there are some prerequisites before you can apply. You have to hold the globally recognised equivalent of a high school diploma and have 1,500 hours of work experience on projects, or have 23 hours of project management education by the time you take the exam.

You can gain the required education hours in a number of ways. Many training providers offer courses that meet the hours requirement and provide you with the information you need to study for the exam successfully.

The exam is a multiple-choice, computer-based question paper. It draws questions only from the latest edition of *A*

Guide to the Project Management Body of Knowledge (PMBOK Guide)®,[21] as it assesses your ability to recall the concepts and terminology and doesn't assess if you are able to apply them.

PMP®

The Project Management Professional (PMP)® credential from PMI is the follow-on certification from CAPM®, aimed at people who already have experience managing project teams. It's not necessary to do the CAPM® first if you meet the eligibility criteria for PMP.

The prerequisites for this credential are either:

- a secondary degree (high school diploma, associate's degree or the global equivalent);
- 7,500 hours leading and directing projects;
- 35 hours of project management education.

or

- a four-year degree;
- 4,500 hours leading and directing projects;
- 35 hours of project management education.

You'll have to evidence both your experience and your education hours (equivalent to a week-long training course, although you don't have to do it all in one go) on your application.

The PMP® credential scheme is accredited by the American National Standards Institute (ANSI) against the International Organization for Standardization (ISO) 17024.

Once you've passed the PMP exam, which is a computer-based multiple-choice exam that you have four hours to complete, you don't have to take it ever again. If you want to maintain your credential you will have to carry out and log continuous professional development time.

Both the CAPM and the PMP credentials are based on the *PMBOK® Guide* and PMI has released a Software Extension[22] to that. This standard provides additional guidance on project management in a software development environment. It aims to bridge the gap between the traditional project management approaches described in the *PMBOK® Guide* and the approaches more commonly used in software development that are more agile and iterative in nature.

Project management credentials have benefits beyond giving you the knowledge required to do the job. Below Agile coach and IT project manager Aaron Porter explains why he opted to go for the PMP® credential.

The two factors in pursuing my PMP were 1) personal achievement, and 2) to be more competitive in the job market. I wasn't expecting more pay at the company where I worked, but I expected the credential to give me more opportunities elsewhere.

The PMP was not my first project management credential, but it was the first that potential employers had heard of. My decision to get my PMP was based primarily on brand recognition, which is kind of funny because my first credential was Marketing Project Manager.

The value of the PMP credential depends upon what you do with it. For me, it has helped me to be more competitive when job hunting, which has resulted in higher paying jobs over time. The benefits are not immediate.

Even more than that, it's helped me pursue other opportunities, such as serving on the Board of Directors of my local PMI chapter, which allowed me to go to regional PMI leadership conferences. It has expanded my professional network which, to be honest, has probably had greater impact on my career than the PMP by itself.

Aaron Porter, USA, beauty and wellness industry

Other credentials from PMI

PMI offers a range of relevant certifications for project managers who wish to specialise or gain a credential that showcases their domain knowledge. The specialist qualifications offered by PMI cover scheduling, risk and Agile project management, so let's look at those next.

PMI Agile Certified Practitioner (PMI-ACP)®

The PMI Agile Certified Practitioner (PMI-ACP)® credential is a specialist qualification that recognises what you know about agile principles and is evidence of your practical experience. It's a fast-growing certification which isn't surprising as agile tools themselves are seeing more and more growth.

It's not specific to one agile approach and the certificate covers Scrum, Kanban, Lean, extreme programming (XP) and test-driven development (TDD). It will round out your experiences and show an employer that you have the versatility to work in multiple agile environments.

To be eligible for the PMI-ACP you have to meet the entry criteria, which are:

- 2,000 hours of general project experience working on teams. If you already hold the PMP® certificate then you'll meet that already, but if you don't then you'll simply have to evidence your experience.

- 1,500 hours working on agile project teams or with agile methodologies. You can't double-count your hours, so in total your experience needs to add up to 3,500 hours.

- 21 contact hours of formal training in agile practices which can be gained through a relevant training course of your choice.

Once you're confident that you can evidence your experience and training you can apply for the exam. It's a three-hour paper delivered through a computer-based test and includes 120 multiple-choice questions.

The exam tests your knowledge of:

- Agile principles and mindset;
- value-driven delivery;
- stakeholder engagement;
- team performance;
- adaptive planning;
- problem detection and resolution;
- continuous improvement.

PMI Scheduling Professional (PMI-SP)®

The PMI Scheduling Professional (PMI-SP)® certificate is for people who understand that building a good project schedule goes beyond using software tools to churn out a Gantt chart.

This qualification will show employers that you have the knowledge and skills to improve the management of schedules and lead on scheduling for your projects. If your projects are complex and scheduling is a challenge, then this could be a good certification for you. In some industries, the role of Scheduler is a defined (and essential) job so if you love this element of project management it is possible to specialise.

To be eligible for the PMI-SP you have to meet these criteria:

- a secondary degree;
- 5,000 hours' experience of project scheduling;
- 40 contact hours of formal education specifically related to scheduling.

Or

- a four-year degree;
- 3,500 hours' experience of project scheduling;

- 30 contact hours of formal education specifically related to scheduling.

These are tough criteria to meet, and you might find that you need to leave it a few years before you can evidence the experience required. Once you're confident that you qualify, you can apply to do the exam. There are 170 questions and you have three-and-a-half hours to complete the exam during the computer-based test. The exam tests your knowledge of five domains:

- schedule strategy;
- schedule planning and development;
- schedule monitoring and controlling;
- schedule closeout;
- stakeholder communications management.

PMI Risk Management Professional (PMI-RMP)®

The PMI Risk Management Professional (PMI-RMP)® credential is a specialist qualification that demonstrates your ability to manage project risk beyond what a 'general' project manager could do. Some industries have a huge focus on risk management, and this certificate could demonstrate to a potential employer that you have the knowledge and skills to act on project risk in a way that would support their business.

To be eligible for the PMI-RMP you have to have spent a lot of time identifying, assessing and managing project risks over the last five consecutive years. There is also a minimum level of education that you need to meet:

- a secondary degree, high school diploma or equivalent;
- at least 4,500 hours spent on risk management tasks in the last five years;
- 40 contact hours of formal education specifically related to risk management.

Or

- a four-year degree, bachelor's degree or equivalent;
- at least 3,000 hours spent on risk management tasks in the last five years;
- 30 contact hours of formal education specifically related to risk management.

The formal education could be a module on your degree course that covered risk management or a course from a recognised training provider. Check the eligibility of any course to make sure it qualifies before you part with money.

If you meet those criteria you can apply for the exam. As with the PMP® exam, it's a multiple-choice paper. There are 170 questions and you have three-and-a-half hours to complete the exam during the computer-based test. The exam tests your knowledge of:

- risk strategy and planning;
- stakeholder engagement;
- risk process facilitation;
- risk monitoring and reporting;
- performing specialised risk analyses.

You can find out more about these PMI certificates and the current entry criteria and assessments on the PMI website.

IPMA® certificates

PMI has a presence almost everywhere, but in some countries there are other active groups that might be more relevant for you. It's important to consider which qualifications and certificates are going to make you the most employable in your market and with employers in your particular area of IT.

The International Project Management Association (IPMA®) is a federation of over 50 membership organisations. Each national association runs its own qualification scheme, but they are all aligned to the international standard framework which categorises qualifications into four levels:

- IPMA® Level A: Certified Projects Director (this is the highest level and is suitable for someone who manages complex project portfolios and programs).

- IPMA® Level B: Certified Senior Project Manager (appropriate for you if you manage complex projects, and requires at least five years of experience).

- IPMA® Level C: Certified Project Manager (designed for people who manage projects of moderate complexity, requiring at least three years of experience).

- IPMA® Level D: Certified Project Management Associate (the entry level qualification which demonstrates your ability to apply project management knowledge in context).

As these levels are internationally recognised, your certificate will be acknowledged by employers in other countries too. This makes the IPMA® framework a good choice if you are planning on spending time working internationally.

In the UK, APM is the local project management association affiliated to IPMA®. It offers a range of qualifications aligned to attainment levels laid out by IPMA®, aimed at professionals with varying levels of experience and skills. These are summarised in Table 5.1.

PRINCE2® Foundation and Practitioner

PRojects IN a Controlled Environment (version 2) is a tried-and-tested project management method that was last updated in 2017. It's built around seven principles, themes and processes as you can see in Table 5.2.

The principles form a framework for good business practice and the processes take you through the project life cycle.

Table 5.1 APM qualifications overview

Qualification	Overview	Eligibility/Audience	Assessed by
APM Project Fundamentals Qualification (PFQ)	PFQ is the introductory qualification. It demonstrates an awareness of the fundamentals of project management terminology and the broad principles of project management.	No prior knowledge required – open to all.	One hour, 60 question multiple-choice paper covering the key elements of the project management life cycle and knowledge areas from the APM Body of Knowledge.
APM Project Management Qualification (PMQ)	PMQ is a knowledge-based qualification covering all elements of project management. It covers knowledge areas from the *APM Body of Knowledge*, which include technical project management skills such as budgeting and cost management, through to interpersonal skills such as conflict management and communication.	You should work in a project-related field. Some pre-existing knowledge is required, such as PFQ or equivalent.	Two options: A three-hour exam. You must answer 10 from 16 questions. Or For PRINCE2® Registered Practitioners there is the option of a two-hour paper that recognises prior learning. You'll have to answer six from ten questions.

(Continued)

Table 5.1 (Continued)

Qualification	Overview	Eligibility/Audience	Assessed by
APM Project Professional Qualification (PPQ)	PPQ is an exam-based qualification that assesses capability. The syllabus is aligned to the APM Competence Framework and is based on the role profile for Intermediate level professionals.	You must currently work in a project-related field and hold the APM PMQ or equivalent.	Three-hour exam with four scenario-based questions. You must pass three core modules (professionalism and managing others, planning and control, governance) and one elective module (choose from project, programme or portfolio management).
APM Practitioner Qualification (PQ)	PQ is the IPMA® Level C certificate.	This is aimed at professionals with at least three years' experience who can demonstrate the ability to manage non-complex projects. You should hold either the PMQ qualification or demonstrate a good understanding of the APM Body of Knowledge and be able to show a commitment to continuous professional development.	Assessed through a residential assessment which looks at 30 criteria including effective planning, teamwork and taking corrective action. You'll have a written test based on a case study and a question on a current issue in project management.

Table 5.1 (Continued)

Qualification	Overview	Eligibility/Audience	Assessed by
			You'll be observed in a group discussing the case study and solving problems.
			There's also an individual interview.
APM Project Risk Management Single Subject Certificate, Level 1 and 2	The Level 1 certificate demonstrates your knowledge of risk management to a level that allows you to contribute to project risk management processes.	This qualification is designed to build on PMQ or equivalent, but there are no formal prerequisites.	Level 1: one-hour exam; 60 multiple-choice questions.
	Level 2 demonstrates your knowledge, understanding and capability to a level that lets you carry out formal project risk management.		Level 2: three-and-a-quarter-hour exam; one compulsory question and two additional questions from a choice of four.

(Continued)

Table 5.1 (Continued)

Qualification	Overview	Eligibility/Audience	Assessed by
Earned Value Management Certification	This qualification was developed jointly with APMG International and APM Earned Value Specific Interest Group. Foundation level covers the basic principles. Practitioner level tests your ability to establish performance measurement baselines for a project, design and evaluate earned value (EV) data collection and interpret the outputs and apply EV across projects.	No prerequisites for Foundation level. Practitioner level is aimed at project professionals who have two years' experience working in an Earned Value Management environment.	Foundation: Multiple-choice, one-hour, 40-question paper. Practitioner: Objective testing, three-hour, four-question paper where you are allowed to take in the Earned Value Management Handbook for reference.

(Continued)

Table 5.1 (Continued)

Qualification	Overview	Eligibility/Audience	Assessed by
Project Planning & Control™	This qualification was developed jointly with APMG International and APM Planning, Monitoring and Control Specific Interest Group. It assesses best practices for project planning and control, based on APM's 'Planning, Scheduling, Monitoring and Control – The Practical Project Management of Time, Cost and Risk.' Foundation is aimed at people who want to understand the basics and be an effective part of the team. Practitioner is aimed at people who need to actively apply the techniques.	No specific prerequisites, although it makes sense to take Foundation before Practitioner to gain an understanding of the terminology and concepts.	Foundation: Multiple-choice, 40-minute exam, 50-question paper. Practitioner: Objective testing, three-hour, eight-question paper where you are allowed to take the reference text into the exam.

Table 5.2 Principles, themes and processes in PRINCE2®

Principle	Theme	Process
Continued business justification	Business case	Starting up a project
Learn from experience	Organisation	Initiating a project
Defined roles and responsibilities	Quality	Managing a stage boundary
Manage by stages	Plans	Closing a project
Manage by exception	Risk	Controlling a stage
Focus on products	Change	Managing product delivery
Tailor to suit the project environment	Progress	Directing a project

The seven themes provide insight into how projects should be managed. They relate to how the principles are put into practice in real life. They are essential to monitoring and controlling a project because they are the things you track. You introduce them at the beginning of a project and then monitor as you go.

PRINCE2® is actually a family of three qualifications: Foundation, Practitioner and Professional.

- **PRINCE2® Foundation:** The basic certification level, which covers the PRINCE2® terminology and methodology, is ideal for project managers, aspiring project managers and any staff members who would play a key role in the project management process.

- **PRINCE2® Practitioner:** The next certification level, PRINCE2® Practitioner is also designed for project managers and aspiring project managers. Passing this exam indicates the individual has sufficient knowledge of how to use and customise PRINCE2® to use in an actual project.

- **PRINCE2® Professional:** The highest level of PRINCE2® certification, PRINCE2® Professional tests your knowledge and ability across all stages of the project life cycle. It requires a two-and-a-half day assessment at a residential assessment centre.

Most candidates in the UK opt to do a combined Foundation/Practitioner course in a classroom, so it's instructor-led training. The course normally takes place over five days with the Foundation exam on the Wednesday. If you are successful you can stay in the classroom for further study on Thursday and take the Practitioner exam on a Friday.

There are also providers offering online learning, weekend courses or you could self-study prior to the exam.

The PRINCE2® 2017 Foundation qualification consists of a one-hour exam, with 60 multiple-choice questions. You must achieve 55 per cent to pass. There are no eligibility criteria although you'll find it easier to understand the concepts if you have some experience of working in a project environment.

The prerequisite for the Practitioner exam is the Foundation certificate or equivalent. The exam is in the objective testing format (a more complicated style of multiple-choice questions). You have 150 minutes to complete the exam and there are 68 questions. The pass rate is also 55 per cent but you can take your official PRINCE2® manual into the exam room as a reference – although there isn't a lot of time to read it.

The pass rates for PRINCE2® exams are published, and this is different from the PMI credentials where the exact pass mark isn't given. Commentators and training providers tend to agree that you need to be looking at routinely getting 75 per cent in your PMI practice exams in order to be sure of passing those.

PRINCE2 Agile®

PRINCE2 Agile® Practitioner is a qualification that demonstrates your ability to apply and tailor the PRINCE2 Agile® methods through a scenario-based assessment.

The certificate assesses your ability to:

- understand the basic concepts of common agile ways of working;

- understand the purpose and context for combining PRINCE2® and agile methods;

- be able to apply or tailor the PRINCE2® principles, themes, processes and approach to an agile environment and flex appropriately.

You'll need to hold another project management qualification before you are eligible to take PRINCE2 Agile® (although this doesn't have to be an agile credential). PRINCE2® Foundation or Practitioner, CAPM®, PMP®, and all levels of the IPMA® scheme are acceptable as prerequisites.

The exam itself follows a similar format to PRINCE2® Practitioner with 50 objective testing questions over a 150 minute exam. You need to get 60 per cent to pass and you can take your official PRINCE2 Agile® guide into the exam room as a reference.

BCS professional certifications in project management

BCS, The Chartered Institute for IT, also offers project management and related qualifications. These are particularly relevant to project professionals working in IT.

These are summarised in Table 5.3.

Table 5.3 BCS professional certifications in project management

Certification	Overview	Eligibility/Audience	Assessed by
IS Project Management Foundation Certificate	This certificate provides an understanding of the principles of project management with techniques to support industry good practice which are complementary to PRINCE2®. Also covers project planning, monitoring and control.	Aimed at anyone involved with or affected by IT projects including users, buyers and directors. There are no entry requirements.	40-question, one-hour multiple-choice-exam.
IS Project Management Higher Certificate	This certificate covers managing plans, people, resources, products, quality, change and risk in an IT environment so it's a comprehensive project management qualification.	Aimed at specialists and managers with in-depth knowledge of their technical area, and is suitable for project management professionals who have previous experience or training in people management, motivation and control. Candidates should have either:	Assessed in three parts: Part 1: During the course candidates need to have a positive assessment to take the written exam. Part 2: A three hour 'closed book' written exam.

(Continued)

Table 5.3 (Continued)

Certification	Overview	Eligibility/Audience	Assessed by
	If you already hold PRINCE2® Practitioner, you can apply for entry to a conversion course which will cut your training time from 80 hours to 40 hours on an accredited programme.	A minimum of four years' experience of management or four years in information systems and have attended an accredited training course before taking the exam or A minimum of three years' experience as a project manager including the use of a recognised methodology. A report should also be submitted detailing the candidate's work experience and practices. This is the direct entry route.	Overall pass rate of 50% as well as 50% pass mark for Question 1. Part 3: A 45 minute oral exam (subject to passing the written exam); this must be taken within 12 months of receipt of the notification of the written exam result.

(Continued)

Table 5.3 (Continued)

Certification	Overview	Eligibility/Audience	Assessed by
Programme and Project Support Office Essentials (PPSO) *Foundation certificate*	Project support roles are increasingly important and this certificate acknowledges this. The qualification assesses an understanding of programme and project organisation structures, planning, documentation, monitoring and reporting.	Aimed at relatively junior team members who are new to project management office work. No entry requirements.	One-hour exam with 40 multiple-choice questions.
Programme and Project Support Office *Advanced practitioner certificate*	You can expect to gain knowledge and understanding of terms of reference and business cases for the programme and project support office with this certificate. Ultimately, you should be able to design, set up and staff the PMO as well as set and maintain service level agreements for business and project level services once you have gone through the training and exam.	Professionals who play a strategic role in the PMO function, such as IT PMO leaders. A basic working knowledge of IT is required, along with two years of relevant work experience. You must hold the Foundation certificate before moving to this level.	Two hour, scenario-based exam which has 15 minutes reading time. There's one mandatory question and a choice of two others from a selection of three.

(Continued)

Table 5.3 (Continued)

Certification	Overview	Eligibility/Audience	Assessed by
Agile Foundation Certificate	This covers the fundamental concepts and values of agile, challenges conventional thinking and application to promote a deeper understanding.	Aimed at both business and IT professionals who want to understand more about agile ways of working. No entry requirements.	One-hour exam with 40 multiple-choice questions.
Agile Practitioner certificate	This certificate is based on 10 modules of the BCS-endorsed ValueFlowQuality, a comprehensive education and learning work-based programme provided by Emergn Education Ltd. The course includes case studies, theory and practical exercises to do in your own team environment. The assignments let you apply your skills to real situations.	Aimed at people who are launching agile in their businesses. There are no entry requirements although candidates are expected to have a basic understanding of Agile which is covered in the Foundation certificate, so it makes sense to do that one first.	There's a two-day accredited training course followed by work-based learning or self-study over the following 2–3 months. Then you'll be eligible to take the three hour, scenario-based exam.

Agile Business Consortium certifications

The Agile Business Consortium has a range of qualifications aimed at people working in an Agile environment, specifically with DSDM® (Dynamic Systems Development Method).

Agile Project Management (AgilePM®), available at Foundation and Practitioner levels, is the most relevant for people starting out in their careers. This is a certification that demonstrates your ability to adopt agile tools and techniques in your workplace. It covers testing, estimating, a variety of agile practices, facilitation and support within an agile project and managing requirements.

The Foundation level is assessed by a 40-minute multiple-choice exam of 50 questions, of which you have to achieve 50 per cent to pass. The Practitioner exam is two-and-a-half hours and follows the objective testing format: the more complicated type of multiple-choice paper also used for PRINCE2® Practitioner. The pass mark is also 50 per cent.

You can go on to take Agile Programme (AgilePgM®) and Agile Portfolio (AgilePfM™) qualifications too, should your career take you in this direction.

CONSIDERATIONS FOR CHOOSING A CERTIFICATION

Exam-based vs. competency

Exam-based qualifications test your ability to understand, apply and recall project management concepts. You don't necessarily need any practical experience to take the exam. Competency-based qualifications showcase your practical experience and you'll need to provide a log of evidence demonstrating you've actually done the job. Both have their place: what's best for you will depend on where you are in your career.

Industry relevance

Look at job adverts for positions in the industry that appeal to you the most and see what kind of qualifications they are asking for. You may notice a trend, in which case it's worth bearing that in mind when you choose what qualification to go for.

Company context

If most of the IT project managers in your company have qualifications from one awarding body, then it makes sense for you to get that one too. Your company may offer financial support for their preferred course or credential but they may choose not to fund other qualifications.

Your study preferences

Consider what format you can study in and what your learning preferences are. If you don't have the option of time away from your job to take a classroom course, you'll have to look for qualifications that are offered online or in a self-paced learning format.

As you can see, there is a wide range of qualifications and professional body schemes to consider. Project management, and IT project management in particular, are not areas that stay still. The knowledge bases that underpin all of these credential schemes are works in progress, continually held under review by their governing body. This means that whichever you go for, you should have confidence in knowing that the standards and documentation have been reviewed by professionals in the field and deemed to be reflective of current best practice.

Each syllabus or body of knowledge is refreshed on a rolling basis so make sure that if you are investing in a text you have chosen the latest version.

Other training courses

Aside from courses that lead to a professionally recognised qualification, there are numerous other opportunities for training that will enhance your career. As an IT project manager, you can study everything from short courses in soft skills to an MBA with a technical project management specialism, and many other courses in between.

It's worth talking to your employer to see what support they offer for training. For project managers early in their career, there is a huge benefit from taking courses that will help you develop your leadership and interpersonal skills as these will strongly influence your career success over time. Take every opportunity for training that is open to you, as you never know what you might learn or who you might meet through the course.

Whatever qualification or course you choose, it's going to support your next move and enhance your CV. You've invested your time and energy into professional development. Whether you're aiming to make your next career move in-house or to move to a new company, the fact that you've committed to improving your skills will help your application shine.

Glen Alleman moved from working in construction and environmental remediation projects to a role in enterprise IT. Below he describes the principles for managing a project successfully and how to define your success criteria.

The five immutable principles for successfully managing any project can be applied across any domain. These principles are:

1. What does 'done' look like in units of measurement meaningful to the decision makers?

2. What's the plan to reach 'done' when needed, for the needed cost?

3. What resources are needed to successfully execute this plan?

4. What impediments will be encountered along the way to 'done'?

5. How will progress to plan be measured?

For example, in both large construction and environmental remediation and enterprise IT, these principles are applicable.

In construction, the physical architecture is the starting point for the project. It's the same for environmental remediation. This architecture is about technical aspects of the project – buildings, bridges, infrastructure. It's also about the programmatic architecture – describing how these items will be built.

In enterprise IT there is usually technical architecture, but rarely a programmatic architecture that describes how the items will be built. You can use it, though. It's possible to define the programmatic architecture: the work processes that increase the probability of arriving on time, on budget, and delivering the capabilities to meet the needs of those paying for the software.

These capabilities are described in Measures of effectiveness and Measures of performance.

- Measures of effectiveness (MOE) are operational measures of success. They are related to delivering the benefit, or operational objectives. They represent the customer's view and expectations.

- Measures of performance (MOP) characterise physical or functional attributes relating to the system operation, measured or estimated under specific conditions. They represent the achievements against the technical specification; the view and expectations of the programmer or engineer.

Both MOE and MOP are derived from statements that answer the question: what capabilities are needed to fulfil the business needs of the customer? This capabilities-based planning paradigm is the basis for the programmatic management of large construction and environmental remediation. Applying this principle to enterprise IT provides insight to what 'done' looks like in units of measurement meaningful to the decision maker, which is sometimes lacking in how IT projects are measured.

Glen Alleman, USA, IT

MOVING UP IN IT PROJECT MANAGEMENT

After spending some time managing projects of some complexity, you'll be thinking about the next phase of your career. Programme management roles are often seen as a natural choice for project managers looking for their next challenge. As businesses get more strategic with project management and start aligning projects together into programmes of work, the need for skilled programme managers grows.

Programme management isn't the same as managing projects and the skills you need are quite different. However, they are certainly aligned and many project managers successfully make the leap into the more strategic and higher-level role of managing a programme of work.

If you want to move into programme management, here are nine skills you can develop during your time as project manager that will help you make the jump to programme level when the time comes.

1. Resource management

In a programme management role there are lots of people, all playing important parts in keeping everything moving in the right direction. At project level you will be used to juggling the resource requirements around within your team so that you've got the right people doing the right things at the right time. On a programme, it's a bigger pool of people.

You'll have to look at the skills required to deliver the programme and work with project managers to resource the projects adequately. Then you might have to take decisions about where to deploy those staff members so that the work gets done in the most efficient way, even if that means taking someone off one project and temporarily asking them to work on another.

It's a huge juggling act and can be quite time consuming. The experience you can build doing similar activities managing teams on projects will definitely help.

2. Stakeholder engagement

Programmes have stakeholders, just like projects do. Hone your skills on your project and you'll be well-placed to use them at programme level.

There is a lot more stakeholder engagement to do at a programme level as the pool of stakeholders is larger and generally people hold more senior roles in the organisation (in other words there is more politics to deal with).

3. Analysis

Analysis is a broad term but really it's the ability to look at lots of different data sources and information and see what's really going on.

You'll have to weed out the opinion, focus on facts and ask challenging questions to get to the root cause of issues. You'll have to dig into the detail and then apply that to the big picture. Being able to assimilate lots of information and condense it into a format that people can understand is important.

Think about how you do that today in your role as a project manager and that might give you some ideas of how you can prove you can do this at a programme level.

4. Decision making

Someone has to make the decisions, and in an IT programme management role, that's often you.

You have to be confident enough to use the information you've received and make the call. There's no hiding in this job.

You make decisions all the time in your project management role, so there's nothing inherently different, except the implications are generally more significant and the buck stops with you.

5. Business acumen

Your programme is delivering some kind of change but there are parameters around that. Use your business acumen skills to understand the commercial aspects of the work beyond the scope of the IT work. You need to be able to think of your programme in the context of other business initiatives and consider the implications for spending money.

This is all about understanding the business case, challenging intelligently and thinking about the cash as if it was your own money on the line. There's possibly also an element of contract negotiation and procurement that perhaps isn't a big part of your project role. Finally, you'll have to manage the programme budget, making sure each project and initiative is adequately financed.

6. Change management

Programmes frequently include an element of business-as-usual work, but mostly they are about changing something. The constituent projects support the overall change the business is looking for. Good change management skills are really important, and this goes beyond knowing how to fill in a change request form and doing the analysis for a project-level change.

This is really about changing behaviour. Programme managers have to bring people along with them, encouraging them to see the vision and to understand why they are going on this journey. And dealing with the inevitable resistance to your plans.

You might work alongside a change manager who can handle these elements, but it's still worth having a broad understanding of change management tools and techniques yourself so that you can assist and support as required.

7. Communication

It should go without saying that programme managers need to be excellent communicators. Again, this is a skill you can hone in a project management role. You'll be able to use all your experience in a programme management job.

The audiences for communication on a programme are quite different, but the analysis and planning for communications have a lot of similarities to project-level communication.

8. Risk management

Risk management is another one of those skills where the title makes it look like you're just doing the same thing as you did on projects but the reality is quite different.

Programme level risk management is not just about rolling up all the project risks into one big log and then asking project managers to stay on top of them. You'll need to link programme level risks to strategic business outcomes, identify issues that will impede other business initiatives and present all of that in a way that ties back to what the executive team really care about. Plus you'll do all the monitoring and corrective action for those risks, as well as supporting project managers with their local issues.

9. The ability to let go

On smaller projects you probably understood a lot of the tasks in minute detail. If you came from a technical or subject matter expert background you might have got stuck doing some of the tasks as well. You can't do that on a programme. First, you are too busy doing programme management and second you can't be close enough to the project detail to be able to get hands on.

You have to acknowledge this and get comfortable with not knowing the minutiae of what is going on. Let it go. You have to trust your project managers and their teams to do what they need to do and to flag problems to you. You have to press on with the confidence that it's all happening, even if you don't know exactly what 'it' is.

Programme management isn't your only choice if you are looking to move on from project management. Portfolio management roles or positions in the Project Management Office are also options. Large-scale industry and construction projects often have larger teams and bigger budgets than programmes of work in smaller companies, so potentially an industry move would let you take on larger and larger IT or business change projects while staying with your project management skill set.

Qualifications to support your career at this stage

Professional qualifications don't stop at project management level. There are qualifications you can achieve to support your ongoing career in a programme management or project office role too.

Common qualifications include:

Managing Successful Programmes (MSP®). MSP® is the AXELOS Best Practice framework to manage complex change through interrelated projects, from the same family as PRINCE2®. You can be certified at Foundation, Practitioner or Advanced Practitioner level. These are assessed through an exam.

Program Management Professional (PgMP®). This credential from PMI is aimed at senior level practitioners managing multiple, related projects in a programme structure. This is assessed through an exam.

APM Registered Project Professional (RPP). This standard from APM demonstrates that you have the competencies required for effective management of projects, programmes and portfolios. It's not aimed specifically at programme managers but it does recognise leadership and experience across the project delivery spectrum, and requires applicants to have a minimum of seven years' experience plus hold an APM project management qualification. The standard is assessed through a written submission and an interview that covers the FIVE Dimensions of Professionalism™: Breadth, Depth, Achievement, Commitment and Accountability. The standard is aligned to the APM Competence Framework.

APM also offers IPMA® Level A and B qualifications through a process of an application, a report and an interview.

Portfolio, Programme and Project Offices (P3O®). P3O® is the AXELOS Best Practice guidance for setting up and maintaining an effective delivery support office. It covers designing, implementing and managing a project office of any kind. Certifications are available at Foundation and Practitioner level and are assessed by exam.

Management of Risk (M_o_R®). This is the AXELOS Best Practice guidance for risk management. It combines principles, an approach and processes to bring together the disciplines required to manage risk effectively at project, programme and portfolio levels. Certifications are available at Foundation and Practitioner level and you're assessed through an exam.

Management of Portfolios (MoP®). MoP® is another Best Practice standard from AXELOS. This one offers guidance on principles, techniques and practices for the framework for delivering projects, decision making and ensuring a return on investment and benefits realisation. As with the other

AXELOS certifications, this one is available at Foundation and Practitioner level and is also assessed through an exam.

Management of Value (MoV®). This Best Practice guidance is aimed at people involved in more senior, strategic levels of project delivery and also at those tasked with improving operational efficiency. It looks at how to get the best out of the work and the most benefit for the investment but it covers more than just reducing costs. Available as Foundation or Practitioner certifications and assessed by an exam.

The Agile Business Consortium offers a range of approved Agile certifications specifically designed for programme managers and experienced project managers working in an agile environment. These include:

Agile Programme Management (AgilePgM®): available at Foundation level only (assessed by a multiple-choice exam) this qualification is aimed at giving you the fundamentals around running an Agile programme. It covers planning, management, control, communication and team structure.

DSDM® Agile Professional: this is an experience-based certification which showcases your expertise in managing projects within a DSDM® (Dynamic Systems Development Method, another Agile method) environment.

IT project management is a truly flexible career. Below Elise Stevens, organisational change management coach and project management podcaster extraordinaire, explains her career path.

When I left university with a degree in electrical engineering I went to work for Qantas on business-type projects. I spent two years working in Germany and then worked for another airline as a senior analyst, then programmer, then team leader and then moved into project management. I was gradually getting more experience and I took a Microsoft Project course.

Then Y2K hit.[23] I was able to move into IT project management roles, grow my skills and through a succession of jobs, became a programme manager. I took the Managing Successful Programmes course to support that. Much of it didn't feel relevant but it did give me a framework for defining a programme as more than the sum of the component projects and other useful tools. I did get value out of it.

In this programme management role I had challenging stakeholders, which reflected what was going on in the organisation at the time. It was a complex political environment and I got to understand the drivers behind people's actions. In particular, people didn't want to collaborate and were happy to work in silos. I used my organisational change skills – everything from showing stakeholders how to use One Note to scheduling to organising testing and training.

Today I'm in an organisational change role and I coach project managers. Technology isn't the answer in situations like that one, where the organisation was broken. I seep into the business and do what's required to ensure projects are successful.

Elise Stevens, Australia, consultant in utilities and other industries

Chartered status

In April 2017 APM became the chartered body for the project profession. The Chartered Project Professional standard (ChPP) was published at the end of 2017 and aims to be:

- achievable by project professionals within a decade of entering the profession;

- open to individuals who are directly involved in the delivery of projects, programmes and portfolios and the associated control functions;

Table 5.4 Competencies required for ChPP

Mandatory competencies for ChPP (all required)	Elective competencies for ChPP (two required)
Team management	Procurement
Conflict management	Contract management
Leadership	Requirements management
Risk and issue management	Solutions development
Consolidated planning	Schedule management
Governance arrangements	Resource management
Stakeholder and communications management	Quality management
Reviews	Transition management
Change control	Resource capacity planning
Budgeting and cost control OR Financial management	Frameworks and methodologies
	Independent assurance
	Asset allocation
	Capability development
	Business case
	Benefits management

- subject to a code of conduct;
- demonstrative of the key competencies required to work in a professional capacity.

Those competencies cover technical knowledge and practical experience across ten mandatory competencies and two of 15 elective competencies, as shown in Table 5.4.

In addition to demonstrating that you have achieved the required standard in the competencies listed in Table 5.4, applicants also need to provide two references related to their project work in the past two years and demonstrate 35 hours of continuous professional development in the past 12 months.

Finally, you have to commit to the Code of Professional Conduct, demonstrate your understanding of what working within an ethical framework looks like, and commit to CPD.

The standard recognises the diverse routes that people take with project management careers and has requirements for candidates to demonstrate technical competence, professional practice and ethics, and continuous professional development. There are three routes to achieving the ChPP designation, depending on your prior certifications:

1. For project professionals with a recognised assessment for technical knowledge. In this case, your professional practice will be assessed by a written submission and interview.
2. For project professionals who hold a recognised assessment for technical knowledge and professional practice. You will need to submit a log of your recent professional development activity and if your application is successful, you will be invited to interview.
3. For project professionals who do not hold a recognised assessment, but are eligible for chartered status. In this case, your technical knowledge will be assessed by interview and your professional practice through a written submission and interview.

There is more information on chartered status, eligibility requirements and how to apply on the APM website.[24]

MOVING OUT OF IT PROJECT MANAGEMENT

The skills you develop working in an IT project management role are highly transferable and can set you in good stead for any role that involves getting work done. Your project management experience will have given you confidence, skills and examples of where you have delivered across a number of technical disciplines that will help you move out of IT project management perhaps into a line or functional role, where you have a team of people working for you on more operational responsibilities.

Equally, you have the opportunity to move out of IT project management into a different industry, but still managing projects. Project management skills are broadly similar across all industries and while your domain knowledge gives you deep insight into how technical projects are run, you can also use your expertise to deliver projects in other domains.

Another option is moving into product management, which could be open to you if you work in an Agile environment (and might still be worth considering even if you don't).

Moving into product management

Project management and product management have some similarities, although they are different jobs. Both roles require you to have excellent communication skills and they both act as a link between one team and another. In a project role you're the link between the project team and the customer. In a product management role, you link the business to the delivery team but with a slightly different focus.

The skills in planning and budgeting as a project manager will help you transition to product management, along with the expertise you'll have gained in managing issues and risks, leading and decision making.

The main difference between the two roles is that a product manager makes decisions over how the project is going to affect the products and the project manager makes decisions over how that is going to be done.

The product manager's role is to set the direction for the project and come up with the solution. They set the strategy for the project and take decisions about the end product. They don't work with the project team to schedule and plan, monitor and control the path to achieving that.

Having said that, on some initiatives to do with their products, they might have to use project management skills because the workload or level of change is too small to involve a dedicated project manager.

Project managers often work with product managers and, especially in Agile teams, it can be an appealing career change. As many of the skills are the same, it can be a relatively straightforward move, although there are some big differences.

The product manager's position is a long-term one. Their involvement starts at the concept and design phase, putting together the business case for a new idea. They act as the project manager's 'customer'. Then they support the project team through delivery. At the end, when the project team disbands and moves on to other initiatives, the product manager is still there, supporting the product through future updates, ongoing customer services and user support and then eventually decommissioning the product when the product life cycle ends. The role has a lot more long-range planning and requires a strategic outlook. There's also a lot more interaction with customers through research and investigation into what they would like the product to evolve into.

There's also a greater focus on sales and marketing, as well as customer service. The financial implications for managing a product are quite different from the project budgeting that you will be used to.

If you enjoyed the fact that you changed projects every so often, working with different teams and on different initiatives, you might miss that in a product manager role.

Product management is definitely a departure from the world of project management, but it's included here as an example of the kinds of role that you can sidestep into, following a successful career as a project manager.

CONTINUOUS PROFESSIONAL DEVELOPMENT

Whatever your role or your plan for developing your career through certifications, take note of the continuous professional development (CPD) requirements or you may lose your ability to reference your qualifications on your CV as they may become invalid.

Being able to demonstrate your CPD is required to maintain your standing with many project management professional bodies. You will be expected to log the activity you did that contributes to your continuing development and in some cases you may be audited on your CPD log.

CPD activities include:

- formal and informal training courses;
- community participation;
- on-the-job professional practice such as internal presentations;
- attending or leading workshops and seminars;
- developing materials for others to learn from – for example, writing articles for industry or internal publications.

Scheme requirements and what counts as CPD differ for each qualification, with some schemes limiting the amount of hours you can claim for particular activities, so always check what is expected of you.

The requirements for professional development relating to some of the more common qualifications are covered in Table 5.5.

Table 5.5 Common CPD requirements in project management

Certification name	CPD requirements	Every...
PMP®	60 Professional Development Units (roughly equal to 60 hours of CPD activity)	Three years
PgMP®	60 Professional Development Units (roughly equal to 60 hours of CPD activity)	Three years
PRINCE2® Practitioner	None: certificate valid for three years at which point you have to re-sit the exam Or Take out AXELOS membership within three months of passing your exam and remain a current member for three years, undertaking 20 points' worth of CPD activity per year across prescribed categories to maintain your standing and avoid re-sitting the exam	Three years
PMI-ACP	30 Professional Development Units (roughly equal to 30 hours of CPD activity)	Three years
CAPM®	None – certificate is valid for five years and you'll need to re-sit the exam after that (or move on to PMP®)	n/a
All APM members	35 hours of informal and formal professional development	One year

Planning your own professional development

Even if you aren't formally obligated to take on CPD it's always a good idea to look at ways each year that you can develop your skills.

Luckily, the project management community is very active and there are lots of events, seminars and websites providing top quality information and learning opportunities for IT project managers.

Here are some options to consider – you can use these even before you begin your career in project management to test out the discipline and see if it feels like a good fit for your future career.

- Attend industry conferences. These tend to be paid events and you may be able to get your employer to sponsor your attendance.

- Attend meet ups, exhibitions and trade shows. These happen in various locations nationally and are normally free to enter, with some exhibitions offering the option of paying to attend specific workshops. There are often some presentations that you can see for free at exhibitions in the main trade show arena. Check out Project Challenge (www.projchallenge.com).

- Read the trade and industry press, both in print and online. If you are a member of a professional organisation, make the most of the publications they offer. If you aren't, see if your PMO has a subscription to a professional journal that you could read. There is a list of websites covering IT project management in Appendix 2.

- Stay connected to the professional groups and key thinkers on social media through blogs and podcasts. There is a list of social media sites covering project management in Appendix 2.

- Take a course in skills related to project management, such as leadership, negotiation or conflict resolution. A short course in this area is unlikely to lead to a qualification, but it will help you develop all-round skills.

- Take a MOOC (a massive open online course, usually offered by a university or similar training provider).

- Take a course in an allied subject such as project management offices, project assurance or information governance, to give breadth to your experience.

- Mentor a colleague if you have experience in a field where other people can benefit from your knowledge. This is a good opportunity for senior project managers looking to prove they can support individuals on a team before moving into a role with direct reports.

- Ask for a mentor. Take advantage of your company's mentor or buddy scheme and ask to be partnered with someone who can support your career through offering you their expertise and being around for you to bounce ideas off.

SUMMARY

There are many opportunities for enthusiastic and experienced IT professionals who want to build a career in project management.

Whether you are looking for your first role, solidifying your experience and demonstrating your skills through qualifications or considering moving up or out into other roles, there are career options that will support your choices.

There is a wide range of qualifications available covering a variety of project management approaches, methods and specialisms. Once you've gained a qualification (and even if you haven't yet) you should demonstrate your commitment to continuous professional development through an ongoing programme of formal and informal learning.

Do this

- Choose a qualification that is appropriate for your career level right now and make the commitment to achieve it within 12 months. Draw up a project plan to schedule out your study time and approach achieving your qualification like a project.

- Plan to attend one formal or informal workshop, seminar or event in the next three months on a topic that lends itself to your CPD.

- Talk to your manager about finding a mentor if you don't already have one.

Share this

I'm going for my [insert qualification of choice] #itpm

I'm committed to ongoing professional development #itpm

Finished the CPD for my #itpm role for the month.

6   A DAY IN THE LIFE OF AN IT PROJECT MANAGER

In this chapter I describe a typical day in the life of an IT project manager.

7.45 a.m. I arrive at my desk. I don't have to be in so early, but I enjoy getting ahead for the day and having time before the rest of the team arrives to plan what needs to get done today. Plus, I avoid the rush hour crush on the train and I get to leave a little earlier normally. One of the great things about project management work is that it is so flexible. As long as your employer is happy that they are seeing the results, you can do the job from broadly anywhere.

The downside is that I have to get up incredibly early to be here at this time, so I browse my emails while I have some breakfast and then clean my teeth and put my make up on in the toilets. The glamour! Luckily there's virtually no one around this early so no one knows this is my normal morning routine.

8.45 a.m. I have a project board meeting at 9.00 a.m., so I make sure I have all the papers that I need. I check I have the conference call organiser pin code so I can dial in the people who aren't in the office. I also need a copy of my project board report and the agenda, which I use to check off who has turned up and annotate the actions from last time.

Many of my colleagues work electronically, taking minutes as they go on a laptop, but I have never got into the habit of doing that, preferring to take notes on paper and then type them up, making clarity from the chaos in my notebook. Also, I know we are meeting in my project sponsor's office and the set up in there isn't great for projecting a presentation or taking notes on a laptop.

9.00 a.m. The project board meeting begins. We're quite early on in formulating this project and the first discussion is around the project scope. There are some queries around how I have documented it, and whether each individual item is in the correct workstream. We also need to get clarity on the workstream owners. My project sponsor chairs the meeting while I take notes and chip in as required.

We move on to discuss the project board report I put together in advance of the meeting. I try to circulate papers for the meeting at least three days in advance so that people have time to read them, and by default we only talk about things that aren't in the report so we don't have the creeping death of going round the room and everyone giving an update.

Today, though, because it's one of the first project board meetings we've had, we do spend a lot of time discussing progress so that everyone is on the same page. I get some clarity around when people are going to do things, which will help me build out a high level Gantt chart for the next meeting. We don't talk about project cost because we run out of time, and we skip over risks and issues – this is a standing agenda item but because we've amended the scope and moved on with the progress, many of the risks on the report need updating before it's worth talking about them.

I quietly send an email to the person I'm supposed to be meeting at 10 a.m., saying that I'm going to be late.

We wrap up with a quick review of the actions from the last meeting, and find that we've covered most of them already. That's why it's handy to do actions at the end of the agenda.

Finally, I confirm the next meeting date with everyone. I have meeting times provisionally booked in my sponsor's diary until the end of the year as she is incredibly busy, and I need to send those same slots out to everyone else so they can also keep the times free.

10.30 a.m. I am late to my next meeting as the project board overran. I am managing two projects at the moment, and this next meeting is with my other project sponsor. He's fine about it, and I'm glad I was able to warn him.

It's quite hard switching from one project to another, but this project has been going for a while and I know it really well. We talk about a major issue with a database that has happened this week and conclude we need some input from the legal team.

We are at a technical junction in the project. We have approval to continue down one technical path, but having further fleshed out the requirements and the solution for that, we've uncovered huge issues that would make it impractical to continue. The project team had a workshop about what to do a fortnight ago, and I've written up the output from that into an options paper. I've given my sponsor three options and put forward a recommendation.

We discuss the rationale behind the thinking and he agrees with my recommendation for the technical solution, with the caveat that he wants more investigation into a certain point. I'm not convinced we can get any closer to what he really wants as there are process, regulatory and technical issues all involved. But I say that I'll talk to the team again.

In most cases, I don't like saying that we can't do something. In IT, with enough money and time we can do pretty much anything. But this is a system change with huge operational implications so as well as the technical stuff I'm also considering the impact of the business change, and that's where the pressure is. In the end, it's his decision and I can only advise what is most likely to be acceptable to end users, practical and cost-effective to build.

At 11.00 a.m. he has to go to another meeting, so I pass by my manager's desk just to check in and say 'hi'.

Back at my desk I catch up on emails from the morning, and send a few myself regarding information I've been asked for in the course of the morning. Then I spend some time working through the major issue so I really understand what is going on – I've got four spreadsheets open and the data visualisation software. I'm not a data analyst by any stretch but needs must. I often find myself doing a task that wouldn't normally be the project manager's role, but in the absence of anyone else with time to do it, it's important to be able to pitch in to keep things moving. Fortunately, right now that seems to be happening less and less.

12.15 p.m. Time for a bit of lunch. I try to get out of the office just to get some fresh air, so I walk to the sandwich shop to buy something to eat.

I still end up eating it at my desk though.

1.00 p.m. I have a pressurised afternoon as I'm going on holiday tomorrow, so I need to be sure that I'm focusing my efforts on what's important for today. I quickly review my To Do list and realise that I haven't prepared the agenda and project dashboard for a meeting next week. I get that ready to send, but I'm interrupted by a colleague asking me about an application program interface (API) issue on a project that was flagged in 2015.

I go through my email archive to see what the conversations were at the time and manage to find something that will help her.

Then the technical lead on one of my projects stops by my desk. He's been on holiday for two weeks, so I catch him up, particularly around the database issue as it's his team who is responsible for this – at least for now. Longer term it will be handed over to a different area, and it's becoming pressing that we get them involved sooner rather than later so they can help out now. He goes away to pick this up.

I take some calls – one from the legal team, others from my project team members. They are all quick, and they all keep the project moving, but together they do take up some time.

I don't manage to get the meeting agenda and other papers out before my next meeting, or update my issue log with the latest on that database problem.

3.00 p.m. I'm in an internal meeting, chaired by the Project Office, with a number of senior leaders and project and programme managers. The purpose is to look over the strategic projects and ensure we understand current dependencies. A lot of the technical work has overlaps in other areas, or on similar customer groups, so it's important that the whole thing is looked at in the round. I do speak to my fellow project and programme managers, but this forum is a good one for making sure everything is transparent.

We share our project timelines and the areas that are impacted, with a view to highlighting where the pinch points will be for our teams. There are a couple of areas where I now know my projects will be impacting, so I can update everyone on those.

This meeting finishes early, so I'm able to get my meeting papers out before my holiday.

4.45 p.m. I leave for the train. At the station I return a phone call from an unhappy project stakeholder. I've sent out some information which I can stand by, but he feels should be showing a different picture. It's not actually his area so neither he nor I can particularly influence the data. We agree to bring this up at the project steering group next week.

On the train I review the emails I didn't get a chance to respond to. There's nothing that can't wait until I'm back from my short break. I try to keep my inbox to under 100 messages and today I'm on around 70 so I'm happy.

I will check my emails later that evening too, and put on my out of office message so people know where I am and when I will be back.

It has been a varied, but average day. A lot of the time has been taken up with stakeholder meetings and talking to my team members, clarifying complex problems for people and making a multitude of small decisions that help keep my projects on track. I haven't looked at my project schedules once, but I have been managing my projects all day.

APPENDIX 1
PROFESSIONAL ASSOCIATIONS

Below are the website details and main published texts about project management from a range of professional associations and providers mentioned in this book.

BCS, The Chartered Institute for IT

Website: www.bcs.org

Main published text about project management: *Project Management for IT-related Projects, Second Edition*

Association for Project Management

Website: www.apm.org.uk

Main published text about project management: *APM Body of Knowledge, Sixth Edition*

Also carries salary survey information.

PMI

Website: www.pmi.org

Main published text about project management: *A Guide to the Project Management Body of Knowledge (PMBOK Guide®) – Sixth Edition*

Also carries salary survey information.

AXELOS

While not strictly a professional association, AXELOS now has a membership scheme for continuing professional development and is the organisation responsible for PRINCE2® and the associated Best Practices.

Website: www.axelos.com

Main published text about project management: *Managing Successful Projects with PRINCE2® 2017 Edition*

Agile Business Consortium

Website: www.agilebusiness.org

Main published text about project management: *The DSDM Agile Project Framework Handbook* (available free online)

International Project Management Association

Website: www.ipma.world

Main published text about project management: Individual member organisations have their own.

Scrum Alliance

Website: https://scrumalliance.org

APPENDIX 2
PROJECT MANAGEMENT
WEBSITES

The professional associations and providers listed in Appendix 1 have detailed and useful websites. Here are some other online resources specifically aimed at IT project managers and leaders.

WEBSITES

www.cio.com
CIO magazine; covers IT leadership topics.

www.enterprisenetworkingplanet.com
Industry news for enterprise IT administrators; some coverage of project management topics.

https://courseconductor.com
Website carrying user reviews of project management training courses; good for choosing a training provider.

www.projectmanagement.com
Community and magazine site from PMI.

LIST OF RELATED BLOGS

www.girlsguidetopm.com
A Girl's Guide to Project Management: Tips & Tricks for Getting Work Done (my blog).

https://thedigitalprojectmanager.com
The Digital Project Manager.

https://bureauofdigital.com/blog
Bureau of Digital blog; aimed mainly at project managers in digital and agency environments.

blog.practicingitpm.com
The Practicing IT Project Manager; carries a useful weekly round-up of project management articles online.

www.patrickmayfield.com
Blog from long-time project management trainer and author, Patrick Mayfield; thought-provoking commentary, mainly around people engagement and change management.

There are also active discussion groups for project managers on LinkedIn and you can follow #pmchat to join in the conversation on Twitter. Facebook users can search for the Project Management Café group to join the conversation there.

APPENDIX 3
PROJECT MANAGEMENT TEMPLATES

Templates are available for many of the project management documents mentioned in this book – you shouldn't ever have to start to create a document from scratch.

You can download over 20 project management templates, checklists and guides from my free resource library.

Go to www.girlsguidetopm.com/welcome-to-the-resource-library for more information.

All the templates are editable documents available for professional use at work. You can amend them to suit your projects and your team, but the terms dictate that you cannot sell them on.

There are a lot of other places online to get project management templates, but the quality varies. You may also find that your colleagues have samples of documents that you can take and edit, already formatted with your company's branding, or that your Project Management Office has a suite of templates that are mandated for your use.

ENDNOTES

1. Maslow, A. H. (1943) 'A Theory of Human Motivation'. *Psychological Review*, 50, 370–396. Available at www.researchhistory.org/2012/06/16/maslows-hierarchy-of-needs (last accessed 8 August 2017).

2. PMI, Pulse of the Profession 2018, Success in Disruptive Times. Available at www.pmi.org/learning/thought-leadership/pulse/pulse-of-the-profession-2018 (last accessed 29 April 2018).

3. See www.girlsguidetopm.com/whats-the-profile-of-a-good-project-manager

4. Available at www.pmi.org/about/ethics/code

5. Available at www.apm.org.uk/about-us/how-apm-is-run/apm-code-of-professional-conduct

6. For more on SFIA®, see www.sfia-online.org

7. In this book I use 'change control' to refer to the process of managing in-project changes such as changes to requirements. 'Change management' is used to mean the wider business practice of facilitating the shift from current practice to new practice in order to achieve a benefit.

8. PRINCE2® uses the term 'Executive' to describe the person who has overall responsibility for ensuring the project meets its objectives. PRINCE2® does not have a specific role called 'sponsor' although it does acknowledge that the sponsor is probably going to be the person in the role

of Executive, or the person who has put the Executive in post.

9. This definition is taken from my book, *Communicating Change: How To Talk About Project Change* (Bookboon, 2017).

10. There's a step-by-step guide for this here: www.girlsguidetopm.com/a-complete-guide-to-raci-rasci-charts

11. There isn't a single definition of what makes a project complex, but complex projects share a number of characteristics including lots of interfaces, ambiguity, uncertainty, emergent solutions, and environments where frequent change is common. A project can be complicated without being complex!

12. See www.agilealliance.org/glossary/backlog

13. See www.scrumalliance.org

14. For more on DSDM®, see the Agile Business Consortium website: www.agilebusiness.org/what-is-dsdm

15. Patton, J. and Economy, P. (2014) *User Story Mapping.* O'Reilly Media.

16. ITIL® is a proprietary form of IT service management. For more on ITIL®, see the AXELOS website: www.axelos.com/best-practice-solutions/itil

17. Burn-up charts work in the same way but instead of showing how much work is still to do, they show how much has been completed, so the graph line goes up instead of down.

18. See www.gartner.com/technology/research/methodologies/research_mq.jsp.

19. This is the result of my own research into how collaboration tools are used on projects. See www.girlsguidetopm.com/how-do-you-use-collaboration-tools-survey-results

20. Excellence, Achievement & Learning Limited: http://eal.org.uk

21. Available here: www.pmi.org/pmbok-guide-standards/ foundational/pmbok/sixth-edition (last accessed 31 December 2017)

22. Available here: www.pmi.org/pmbok-guide-standards/ foundational/pmbok/software-extension-5th-edition (last accessed 8 August 2017)

23. A historical note: Y2K (the 'millennium bug') was a perceived issue with software because many programs were created with dates hard coded as 19xx. There was concern that when 2000 came around, the software wouldn't be able to deal with the date change and software failures would ensue. At the time, people were concerned about planes falling out of the sky and similar meltdowns. This was a busy time for IT project managers. Y2K passed largely without incident.

24. See www.apm.org.uk/chartered/pp

INDEX